M000205093

Bay Area
Mountain Bike Trails

45 Mountain Bike Rides
Throughout the San Francisco Bay Area

by
Conrad J. Boisvert

Penngrove Publications
P.O. Box 798
Pescadero, CA 94060
www.penngrovepublications.com

For my sister, Grace

Bay Area Mountain Bike Trails, 2nd Edition
Copyright © 2004 by CONRAD J. BOISVERT

Library of Congress Control Number: 2003098686
International Standard Book Number: 0-9621694-6-3

Cover photograph by Conrad Boisvert
Taken on Indian Creek Trail in Monte Bello Open Space Preserve
Cyclists: Judie Boisvert and John Gray

Photographs in the book were taken by Conrad Boisvert

Printed in the United States of America

First printing, November 1993
Second printing, September 1995
Third printing, March 2000
Fourth printing, August 2002
Second edition, August 2004

𝓟enngrove Publications
P.O. Box 798
Pescadero, CA 94060
www.penngrovepublications.com

TABLE OF CONTENTS

Hit the Trails of the Bay Area! 5
Regions of the Bay Area 6
The San Francisco Bay Area 7
How to Use This Book 8

The South Bay **10**
  1. San Jose — Grant Ranch County Park 11
  2. Los Gatos — St. Joseph's Hill Open Space Preserve 14
  3. Los Gatos — Sierra Azul Open Space Preserve 17
  4. Morgan Hill — Henry Coe State Park — Middle Ridge Loop . 20
  5. Gilroy — Henry Coe State Park — Wilson Ranch Loop 23
  6. Aptos — Forest of Nisene Marks State Park —
     Five Finger Falls Bike & Hike 27
  7. Aptos — Forest of Nisene Marks State Park —
     Sand Point Overlook 31
  8. Soquel — Soquel Demonstration Forest 34
  9. Felton — Henry Cowell Redwoods State Park 37
 10. Davenport — Big Basin Redwoods State Park
     — Berry Creek Falls Bike & Hike.................... 40
 11. Saratoga — Big Basin Redwoods State Park............... 44
 12. Santa Cruz — Wilder Ranch State Park 48
 13. Santa Cruz — Wilder Ranch State Park,
     UC Santa Cruz, and Pogonip Preserve................ 51

The San Francisco Peninsula **54**
 14. Palo Alto — Arastradero Preserve..................... 55
 15. Cupertino — Monte Bello Open Space Preserve........... 58
 16. Cupertino — Fremont Older Open Space Preserve......... 61
 17. Pescadero — Butano State Park 64
 18. Woodside — El Corte de Madera Open Space Preserve...... 67
 19. Woodside — Purisima Creek Redwoods
     Open Space Preserve 70
 20. Loma Mar — Old Haul Road 73
 21. Palo Alto — Russian Ridge Open Space Preserve 76
 22. Palo Alto — Skyline Ridge Open Space Preserve........... 79
 23. Saratoga — Saratoga Gap and Long Ridge Preserves........ 82
 24. Portola Valley — Alpine Road and Windy Hill 85

The East Bay. **88**
 25. San Leandro — Anthony Chabot Regional Park........... 89
 26. San Leandro — Redwood Regional Park 92
 27. Pleasanton — Pleasanton Ridge Regional Park............ 95
 28. Newark — Coyote Hills Regional Park................. 98
 29. Livermore — Morgan Territory Regional Preserve 101
 30. Sunol — Sunol-Ohlone Regional Wilderness 104
 31. Lafayette — Briones Regional Park 107
 32. Berkeley — Tilden and Wildcat Canyon Regional Parks 110

REGIONS OF THE BAY AREA

The South Bay   Rides 1-13

The South Bay region is centered on San Jose. Near to San Jose is the rugged former ranchland of Grant Ranch in the foothills below Mt. Hamilton. The chaparral-covered mountains of the Sierra Azul Open Space Preserve and the historic St. Joseph's Hill are close to Los Gatos. More distant are the primitive and remote Henry Coe State Park, the redwood forests and steep hillsides of The Forest of Nisene Marks, Henry Cowell Redwoods, and Big Basin State Parks, and the single-track trails of Soquel Demonstration Forest and Wilder Ranch State Park.

The Peninsula   Rides 14-24

Mountain biking on the Peninsula is primarily available in the vast amount of public land administered by the Midpeninsula Regional Open Space District. Monte Bello, Fremont Older, Long Ridge, Russian Ridge, Skyline Ridge, El Corte de Madera, Windy Hill, and Purisima Creek Redwoods are preserves in the Santa Cruz Mountains that are open to mountain biking. Butano State Park, Pescadero County Park, and Arastradero Preserve add to the wealth of opportunities for trail exploration and recreation.

The East Bay   Rides 25-34

Whereas the East Bay is often the hottest and driest of Bay Area regions in the summer, its beauty in the spring and fall is unrivaled. In the springtime, when the grass-covered slopes are green from the winter moisture and the creeks are flowing with mountain run-off, the grandeur of the East Bay is hard to beat. The cooling days of the fall bring the golden colors of the season to their peak brilliance. Although the hills of the East Bay are typically not as high as those along the coast, Mt. Diablo remains among the highest in the entire Bay Area.

The North Bay   Rides 35-45

In many ways, it should come as no surprise that the North Bay was the birthplace of the mountain bike. The endless miles of trails around Mt. Tamalpais created the need for a rugged all-terrain bike and the resourceful trail users there developed it. The scenery from the trails on and around the mountain, and in the Marin Headlands, can be quite sensational. At each turn, views alternate between scenes of the Pacific Ocean, Sausalito, Angel Island, the Golden Gate Bridge, and the magnificent skyline of San Francisco. Farther north, Annadel State Park, Samuel P. Taylor State Park, Point Reyes, and China Camp provide more opportunities to ride and to exult.

THE SAN FRANCISCO BAY AREA

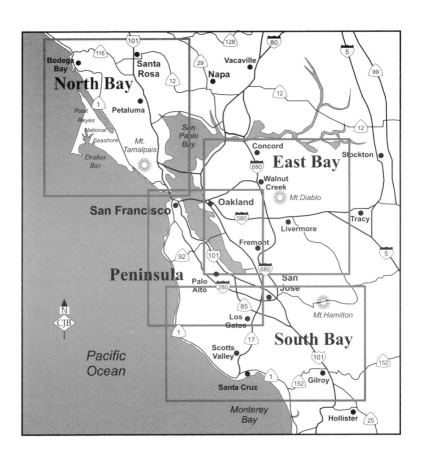

The South Bay. . . . . .Page 10

The San Francisco Peninsula .Page 54

The East Bay. . . . . .Page 88

The North Bay. . . . . .Page 120

HOW TO USE THIS BOOK

Understanding the Ride Parameters

At the beginning of each ride description is a short list of ride parameters. These are intended to give you a brief summary of that particular ride and to permit you to quickly select the ride that most suits what you are looking for.

Difficulty Rating — Reflects the overall difficulty of the ride, in terms of the physical effort needed. There are three levels: *Easy*, *Moderate*, and *Difficult*. The rating results from an evaluation of both the distance and elevation gain for the ride and is also influenced by the steepness of the climbs.

Skill Level — Refers to the level of technical mountain biking skills that the ride requires. Skill levels are designated as *Non-technical*, *Somewhat technical* and *Very technical*. Rides with a *Non-technical* skill level usually have wide and smooth trails and modest grades along the climbs and descents. Those which require *Very technical* skills can have narrow trails with steep and bumpy conditions and may also have tight switchbacks to contend with.

Elevation Gain — combines the total elevation gain for all the hills along the route.

Total Distance — indicates the total length of the ride, including roads.

Off-Road Distance — indicates the mileage along trails and fire roads and along paved pathways, but not mileage along roads with car traffic.

Riding Time — gives an indication of how much time to allow for the ride. Keep in mind however, that this does not include extended stops for sightseeing, eating, or rests. The riding time usually assumes a moderate pace of about 4-7 miles an hour for most types of terrain.

About the Ride

This section outlines a general description of the ride along with any interesting background or historical information about the area. The general route to be followed is explained, although the details are covered more fully in the *Ride Details and Mile Markers* section. A brief description of the terrain of the trails is also explained, including the steepness of the grades, the nature of the trails (bumpy or rocky, narrow or wide). Whether the trail signs are easy to follow is also indicated, as well as whether the trails are sunny or shady or whether some special items of interest are important.

Starting Point

The exact place to start the ride is described, along with detailed directions explaining how to get there. Ideally, but not always, rides are started at locations where free parking is readily available and where restrooms and information boards are located. Typically the starting points are also easily recognizable places, simplifying the situation for a group of people meeting to ride together. On maps, the starting points are indicated on the map with an asterisk ✷.

Elevation Profile

The elevation profile provides a detailed view of the hills along the route. It not only previews the climbing for you before you do the ride, but can be useful on the ride to help you anticipate the terrain ahead of you. Grades (in percent) for significant hill climbs are often indicated. A 10% grade is one that has about 500 vertical feet of elevation gain for each mile of distance.

Map

Each ride has a map associated with it indicating the route. Roads and trails are indicated with various degrees of thickness. The thickest lines indicate paved roads with car traffic. The medium lines are for fire roads and some trails that are wide. The thinnest lines represent hiking trails and single-track. While the maps are drawn as accurately as possible, sometimes trails are closed or new ones are developed, so it is advisable to get new trail maps, if they are available, when visiting an unfamiliar place. See key for common symbols used on the maps.

MAP KEY

● city or town name
■ point of interest
P parking
▲ campground
✷ ride start point
→ ride direction
↘ gate
⌐ ¬ park/preserve boundary
⌊ ⌋
🔆 mountain peak

Ride Details and Mile Markers

Directions for the route are described along with elapsed distances. You don't necessarily need a cycle computer for following the route, since the markers come at frequent intervals and you will quickly learn to estimate distances accurately enough. The required turns to take are clearly indicated. Special sights or points of interest along the way are also indicated.

The South Bay

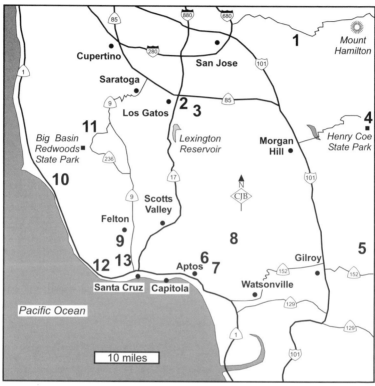

Ride 1.   San Jose — Grant Ranch .... Page 11
Ride 2.   Los Gatos — St. Joseph's Hill. .... Page 14
Ride 3.   Los Gatos — Sierra Azul .... Page 17
Ride 4.   Morgan Hill — Henry Coe State Park —
          Middle Ridge Loop .... Page 20
Ride 5.   Gilroy — Henry Coe State Park — Wilson Ranch Loop . Page 23
Ride 6.   Aptos — Forest of Nisene Marks — Five Finger Falls
          Bike and Hike .... Page 27
Ride 7.   Aptos — Forest of Nisene Marks — Sand Point Overlook Page 31
Ride 8.   Soquel — Soquel Demonstration Forest .... Page 34
Ride 9.   Felton — Henry Cowell Redwoods. .... Page 37
Ride 10. Davenport — Big Basin — Berry Creek Falls
          Bike & Hike .... Page 40
Ride 11. Saratoga — Big Basin Redwoods .... Page 44
Ride 12. Santa Cruz — Wilder Ranch .... Page 48
Ride 13. Santa Cruz — Wilder Ranch, UCSC, and
          Pogonip Preserve .... Page 51

1

San Jose
Grant Ranch County Park

Difficulty Rating: *Difficult*	**Total Distance:** *16 miles*
Skill Level: *Somewhat technical*	**Off-Road Distance:** *16 miles*
Elevation Gain: *1,900 feet*	**Riding Time:** *3 hours*

About the Ride

In the foothills below Mt. Hamilton, just a short distance from central San Jose, lies the former Grant Ranch. Once an operating ranch and now a county park, *Grant Ranch County Park* offers challenging mountain biking along wide fire roads through pastures populated with grazing livestock. While the park is not entirely open to bicycles, this route will lead you through that portion of the park where biking is permitted.

After a short 1-mile stretch of trail leading away from the parking area, a rather steep section gets the heart pounding. Once past Eagle Lake, more climbing along Digger Pine Trail and Bohnhoff Trail leads to Mt. Hamilton Road, across which the trail continues. Cañada de Pala Trail leads through a high meadow and to an old line shack formerly used by ranch hands. After this, the route is nearly all downhill back to park headquarters where it began.

Almost 2,000 feet of climbing on some rather steep trails makes this ride a difficult one. The trails are wide and usually the surfaces are relatively smooth, so intermediate-level skills are all that are necessary.

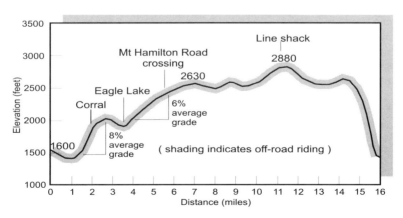

Starting Point

To get to *Grant Ranch County Park*, take Highway 680 east of San Jose and get off at the exit for Alum Rock Avenue. Proceed east on Alum Rock for about 2 miles and then turn right onto Mt. Hamilton Road. Continue for about 8 miles to the park and enter it at the main entrance. Go all the way through and to the left side where the visitor center and the trailhead are located.

Mile Markers

0.0   Proceed EAST from the parking area and go past two livestock gates to the Hotel Trail.

0.3   Turn RIGHT onto Lower Hotel Trail and begin a short descent.

1.0   Continue STRAIGHT at the intersection with Barn Trail on the right side.

1.6   Continue past the livestock gate.

1.8   Continue STRAIGHT through the corral.

1.9   Steep uphill section.

2.3   Trail intersection on the left side.

3.5   Eagle Lake on the right side. Bear LEFT and descend into the canyon along Foothill Trail.

4.6   Turn LEFT onto Bonhoff Trail and begin steep uphill section.

5.5   Continue STRAIGHT across Mt. Hamilton Road and get on Cañada de Pala Trail at the Twin Gates trailhead

6.0   Yerba Buena Trail intersection on the left side.

7.0   Bench on the left side with views to the Santa Clara Valley.

7.3   Continue STRAIGHT at the intersection with Los Huecos Trail on the left side.

7.8   Continue STRAIGHT at the intersection with Halls Valley Trail on the left side.

8.3   Bear LEFT to stay on Cañada de Pala Trail.

10.0   Pass the old line shack on the left side and then bear RIGHT to get on Pala Seca Trail.

12.2   Bear LEFT at the trail intersection to get back on Cañada de Pala Trail.

13.0   Turn RIGHT onto Los Huecos Trail and begin a sometimes steep descent.

14.1   Gate.

15.1   Turn LEFT to stay on the trail as it goes around the lake.

15.4   Continue STRAIGHT through the parking lot and turn RIGHT onto Mt. Hamilton Road.

15.8   Turn LEFT into the main park entrance.

16.2   End of the ride at the parking area.

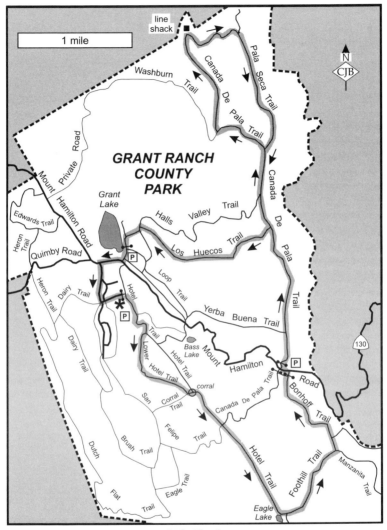

Ride No. 1

2 Los Gatos
St. Joseph's Hill Open Space Preserve

Difficulty Rating: *Moderate*   **Total Distance:** *6 miles*
Skill Level: *Somewhat technical* **Off-Road Distance:** *5 miles*
Elevation Gain: *700 feet*   **Riding Time:** *1-2 hours*

About the Ride

Situated just a short distance from central Los Gatos, *St. Joseph's Hill Open Space Preserve* is quite popular with local hikers, runners and cyclists. Formerly owned by the *California Society of the Province of Jesus*, the land is now administered by the Midpeninsula Regional Open Space District.

The route begins in Los Gatos at Los Gatos High School where parking is plentiful. After leaving the surface roads, Jones Trail leads you into the preserve and some steep climbs along Novitiate Trail and Manzanita Trail will take you to the top of the hill where you will be rewarded with sweeping views of the South Bay to the north, Lexington Reservoir to the south and the Sierra Azul Mountains to the southeast. Manzanita Trail leads down off the hill back to Jones Trail and from there to Alma Bridge Road for a short stretch along pavement to Los Gatos Creek Trail and the easy return to Los Gatos.

While the ride is quite short, the trails are rather steep and rocky in many places. Because of this, the ride is rated as a moderate ride, even though many intermediate riders might consider it easy because of its short length.

Starting Point

Start the ride at Los Gatos High School in Los Gatos. Take the Saratoga Avenue (Highway 9) exit off Highway 17 and proceed east on Saratoga Avenue to where it ends at Los Gatos Boulevard. Turn right onto Los Gatos Boulevard (which becomes East Main Street) and follow it for about ½ mile to the high school, located on the right side. Park nearby and begin the mileage on East Main Street, in front of the school.

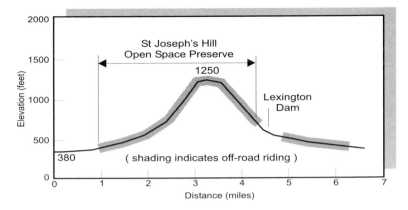

(shading indicates off-road riding)

Mile Markers

0.0   Proceed WEST on East Main Street, heading toward central Los Gatos.

0.2   Turn LEFT onto College Avenue.

0.6   Turn RIGHT onto Jones Road.

0.8   At the end of Jones Road, proceed past the gate and onto Jones Trail.

1.5   Turn LEFT onto Novitiate Trail and begin climbing.

1.8   Bear LEFT at the intersection with Manzanita Trail on the right side to continue on Novitiate Trail.

2.0   At the intersection of four trails, proceed STRAIGHT onto Manzanita Trail, the middle of the three trail possibilities, toward the hilltop.

2.5   At the top of the hill there are views of Lexington Reservoir far below. The meadow on the right side of the trail is where the Novitiate grew its grapes for use in the wines it made. Proceed straight ahead down the hill along Manzanita Trail.

3.0   At the intersection of four trails, bear LEFT to stay on Manzanita Trail.

3.7   Turn LEFT onto Novitiate Trail.

3.9   Turn LEFT to get back on Jones Trail.

4.4   Proceed past the gate and turn RIGHT onto Alma Bridge Road.

4.5   Turn RIGHT before the dam to get onto Los Gatos Creek Trail for the return to Los Gatos.

6.4   At the end of the trail, proceed past the gate and turn RIGHT onto East Los Gatos Boulevard.

6.7   End of the ride at the high school.

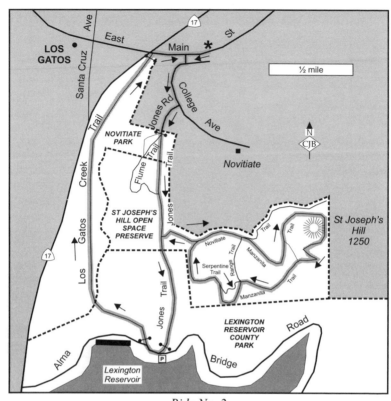

Ride No. 2

Lexington Reservoir as seen from St. Joseph's Hill

3 Los Gatos
Sierra Azul Open Space Preserve

Difficulty Rating: *Difficult*	**Total Distance:** *16 miles*
Skill Level: *Somewhat technical*	**Off-Road Distance:** *16 miles*
Elevation Gain: *3,000 feet*	**Riding Time:** *3 hours*

About the Ride

Located in the Santa Cruz Mountains just outside of Los Gatos, *Sierra Azul Open Space Preserve* ("Sierra Azul" is Spanish for "blue mountains") stretches all the way from Lexington Reservoir to Mt. Umunhum. Fire roads and some single-track lead through the preserve along scrub-covered ridges to elevations as high as 2,860 feet where there are panoramic views of the Santa Clara Valley and the Santa Cruz Mountains. This ride covers most of the preserve and is very strenuous. Even though most of the trails are wide, challenges can be found for even the most experienced riders.

The route begins in Los Gatos and leads through quiet residential neighborhoods along a steady climb on surface roads to the trailhead at the hilltop of Kennedy Road. After a brief flat section in the beginning, the fire road then climbs steeply and leads to the top of the ridge. Rolling terrain along the ridgeline is followed by a long downhill back to Alma Bridge Road. A brief stretch along the road leads to the easy cruise back to town along Los Gatos Creek Trail.

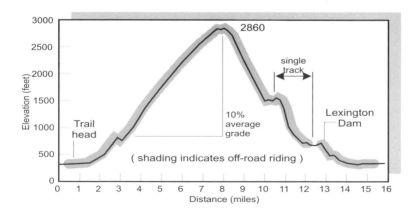

Starting Point

Start the ride at Los Gatos High School in Los Gatos. Take the Saratoga Avenue (Highway 9) exit off Highway 17 and proceed east on Saratoga Avenue to where it ends at Los Gatos Boulevard. Turn right onto Los Gatos Boulevard (which becomes East Main Street) and follow it for about ½ mile to the high school, located on the right side. Park in the back of the school or nearby.

Mile Markers

0.0   Proceed EAST on East Main Street, heading away from central Los Gatos.

0.5   Continue STRAIGHT at the intersection with Los Gatos-Saratoga Avenue on the left side.

0.7   Turn RIGHT onto Kennedy Road.

3.0   At the crest of Kennedy Road, turn RIGHT and go past the gate into Sierra Azul onto Kennedy Trail.

3.6   Steep climbing begins.

5.6   False summit — elevation is 2,580 feet.

5.7   Continue STRAIGHT at the trail intersection with Priest Rock Trail (also known as "Dogmeat") on the right side.

7.4   Turn RIGHT onto Limekiln Trail (also known as "Power Lines").

10.4   Continue STRAIGHT at the major intersection where four trails come together to stay on Limekiln Trail (also known as "Overgrown").

10.7   Continue past the gate.

12.2   Exit the preserve and turn RIGHT onto Alma Bridge Road.

12.7   Turn RIGHT before the dam to get onto Los Gatos Creek Trail for the return to Los Gatos.

14.7   At the end of the trail, proceed past the gate and turn RIGHT onto East Los Gatos Boulevard.

15.0   End of the ride at the high school.

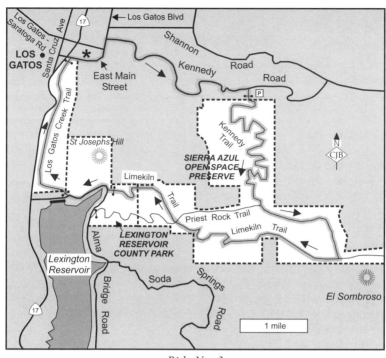

Ride No. 3

Along the ridgeline in Sierra Azul

4 Morgan Hill
Henry Coe State Park — Middle Ridge Loop

Difficulty Rating: *Difficult*	**Total Distance:** *10 miles*
Skill Level: *Very technical*	**Off-Road Distance:** *10 miles*
Elevation Gain: *2,100 feet*	**Riding Time:** *2 hours*

About the Ride

About 12 miles east of Morgan Hill lies *Henry Coe State Park*, one of the largest and most remote of all the parks in the Bay Area. Its remoteness is part of its mystique. Unusual wildlife is often encountered here. It is not at all uncommon to see wild pigs, turkeys or golden eagles in and around the park. Snakes and poison oak are common too, so it is important to be careful when visiting the park.

This ride leads around the northern section of the park, the most popular area for visitors. Park headquarters, where there is an informative visitor center and many relics of the former operating ranch, is the starting point. A brief visit will acquaint you with the park and help you to get the most out of your visit.

The route leads along a fire road away from the visitor center and climbs a short hill to a monument for Henry Coe, the former owner of the ranch. After a small descent and then another short climb, the route will take you onto Middle Ridge Trail. The steep descent along this narrow single-track has numerous switchbacks and offers plenty of challenge for all skill levels. At the bottom, at Poverty Flat, there is a stream crossing and then the return to park headquarters along a rather steep climb on a fire road.

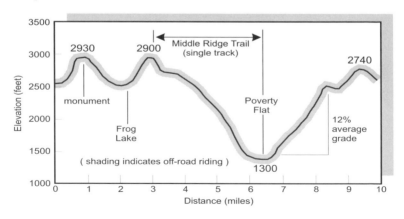

Starting Point

Start the ride at park headquarters in *Henry Coe State Park*. To get there, take Highway 101 south from San Jose to Morgan Hill and get off at the exit for East Dunne Avenue. Follow East Dunne Avenue east for about 12 miles up into the hills. At the end of the road is the park where there is a nominal fee for day-use parking.

Mile Markers

0.0 Begin by taking the fire road across the road from the visitor center and begin climbing.

0.5 Turn LEFT at the junction of two fire roads and continue climbing toward the monument along Hobbs Road.

1.0 Bear LEFT at the junction with the trail to Frog Lake to stay on Hobbs Road.

2.2 Frog Lake is to the right.

2.7 Crest of the hill — begin downhill section.

3.0 Turn RIGHT onto Middle Ridge Trail.

3.2 Bear LEFT to stay on Middle Ridge Trail.

4.0 Begin steep and narrow descent.

4.4 Bear LEFT at trail split and continue toward Poverty Flat.

6.4 Cross over stream.

6.5 Cross stream and turn RIGHT onto Poverty Flat Road. Begin climb toward park headquarters.

8.1 Bear RIGHT onto Manzanita Point Road.

9.8 End of the ride at park headquarters.

The historic Coe Ranch

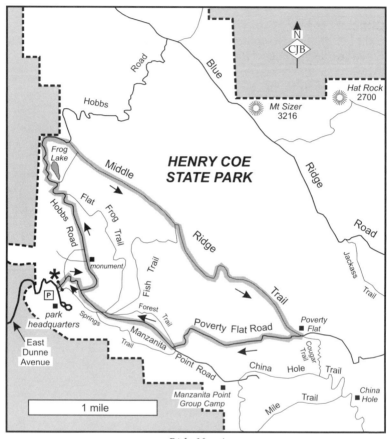

Ride No. 4

Bay Area Mountain Bike Trails

5 Gilroy
Henry Coe State Park — Wilson Ranch Loop

Difficulty Rating: *Difficult*	**Total Distance:** *17 miles*
Skill Level: *Somewhat technical*	**Off-Road Distance:** *15 miles*
Elevation Gain: *2,000 feet*	**Riding Time:** *3-4 hours*

About the Ride

Henry Coe State Park lies about 12 miles east of Morgan Hill and Gilroy in the southernmost part of Santa Clara County. The former operating ranch of Henry Coe, the park today is one of the largest state parks in northern California and continues to expand as lands are opportunistically acquired.

The southern section of the park, while not visited as much as the northern part, is becoming more and more popular as word of its special qualities spreads. This ride consists of a loop around a small part of the southern section. There is an entry into this area near the once-famous Gilroy Hot Springs, situated at the end of Gilroy Hot Springs Road. There is no visitor center in this part of Henry Coe and no drinkable water is available, so it is important to bring adequate supplies with you.

The route follows from the recently-opened Hunting Hollow parking area along Gilroy Hot Springs Road to a gated entrance at the end of the road. From there, a fire road leads into the park and climbs steeply to another fire road which goes along the ridgeline with views in both directions. At the top, just before the fire road descends toward Kelly Lake, the route turns onto Wasno Road, another fire road along another ridge. Wasno Road leads down slightly into a meadow with a lily-covered pond. Beyond this, the route continues to Wilson Ranch with several dilapidated structures remaining to remind the visitor of what it might have been like on a remote cattle ranch. From Wilson Ranch, the trail changes to a narrow single-track running along the slopes of the hillsides, offering spectacular views on the way back to Hunting Hollow.

The trails are well-marked and easy to follow. Summers can be very hot and dry, so be prepared and avoid the hottest days. Springtime is perhaps the best time to visit, when the creeks are flowing and the wildflowers and buckeye trees are in full bloom.

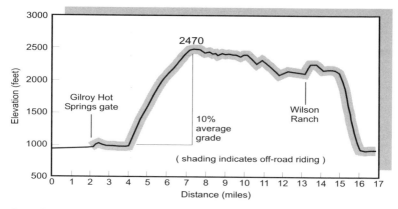

Starting Point

Follow Highway 101 south from San Jose to Gilroy. Exit at Leavesley Road and turn left to head east on Leavesley Road, away from central Gilroy. After about 2 miles, turn left onto New Avenue and then right onto Roop Road which ultimately becomes Gilroy Hot Springs Road. The parking area at Hunting Hollow is less than a mile after the Cañada Road intersection.

Mile Markers

0.0   Turn RIGHT out of the Hunting Hollow parking area onto Gilroy Hot Springs Road.

2.0   The road ends at a bridge leading into Gilroy Hot Springs (private.) Turn RIGHT before the bridge and go past the gate onto the fire road into Henry Coe State Park.

2.1   Bear LEFT at the trail split and cross creek.

2.8   Top of a small hill with views of the Gilroy Hot Springs in the distance on the left side side.

4.0   Anza Trail intersection on the right side.

5.3   Coit Camp and corral on the left side.

6.0   Turn RIGHT at major fire road intersection to stay on Coit Road heading toward Kelly Lake.

6.3   Continue STRAIGHT at intersection with Cross Canyon Trail.

7.5   Train intersection on the right side.

8.0   Turn RIGHT onto Wasno Road heading toward Wilson Camp.

8.6   Bear LEFT at the intersection with Jackson Road on the right side.

9.0   Kelly Lake Trail intersection on the left side.

10.8   Turn RIGHT sharply onto Wagon Road heading toward Wilson Camp and Hunting Hollow.

12.4   Bear LEFT to stay on Wagon Road toward Wilson Camp.

- 13.2 Bear RIGHT at major intersection to stay on Wagon Road (Vasquez Road is on the left side.)
- 13.4 Arrive at Wilson Ranch, now deserted. Look for a small trail to the RIGHT side of the ranch buildings. It leads around to the back of the buildings and takes you to The Bowl Trail. Turn RIGHT onto The Bowl Trail.
- 14.3 Bear LEFT onto the Lyman Wilson Ridge Trail.
- 15.4 Continue past the cattle gate.
- 16.4 Continue past another cattle gate and turn RIGHT onto the fire road in Hunting Hollow.
- 17.1 End of the ride at the Hunting Hollow parking area.

Wilson Ranch

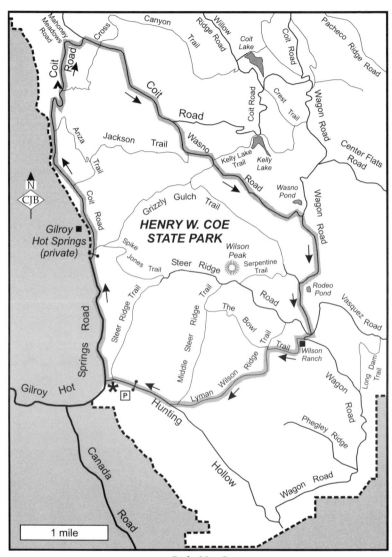

Ride No. 5

6 Aptos
Forest of Nisene Marks State Park —
Five Finger Falls Bike & Hike

Difficulty Rating: *Easy*	**Total Bike Distance:** *8 miles*
Skill Level: *Non-technical*	**Total Hike Distance:** *6 miles*
Bike Elevation Gain: *500 feet*	**Riding Time:** *1 hour*
Hike Elevation Gain: *1,500 feet*	**Hiking Time:** *3 hours*

About the Ride and Hike

In October of 1989, while a baseball World Series game was just about to begin in Oakland, the earth shook throughout the Bay Area. Registering 7.1 on the Richter scale, with its epicenter about a mile below the surface of a point located within *The Forest of Nisene Marks State Park* in Aptos, the quake shook the entire county of Santa Cruz. Initially, earthquake experts believed the epicenter was located along Aptos Creek Fire Road and a marker was erected to designate the approximate spot. After more study, it was decided that the actual location was more likely to be somewhat off the fire road and along Aptos Creek Trail. The marker was moved to that location where it remains.

This combination ride and hike leads into *The Forest of Nisene Marks State Park* along Aptos Creek Fire Road. After biking in along a fairly gentle uphill grade for about 4½ miles, a bike rack is located. The location of the bike rack is at the trailhead for Aptos Creek Trail which leads to the epicenter marker about a half mile in. Bicycles are not permitted along this trail. Continuing on that same trail for about 2½ miles more, the route leads to Five Finger Falls. Since the falls is at the end of the trail, the return back is the along same route.

Stream crossings, which require some rock hopping, and muddy conditions, which often occur in winter and springtime, suggest the need for sturdy hiking boots. Bike shoes are not the best idea for the hike. Be sure to bring along a lock for securing your bike to the rack.

Starting Point

To get to the starting point, take Highway 1 south from Santa Cruz. Get off in Aptos at the Seacliff Beach — Aptos exit and turn left onto State Park Drive. Turn right onto Soquel Drive and follow it under a railroad bridge, after which will be Aptos Creek Road on the left side. Park near this intersection to begin the ride.

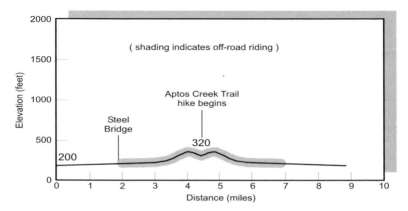

Mile Markers

0.0 Proceed away from Soquel Drive along Aptos Creek Road.

0.4 Bridge over Mangel's Creek.

1.2 Day use pay booth — no charge for bicycles.

2.1 George's Picnic Area on the right side.

2.2 Continue STRAIGHT over Steel Bridge.

3.2 Porter Family Picnic Area on the right side — continue past the gate onto Aptos Creek Fire Road.

3.6 The remains of the Loma Prieta Mill site is on the left side.

4.3 Cross bridge over creek and look for the bike rack on the right side. Lock your bike here and follow Aptos Creek Trail on the right side as it crosses over the creek and winds its way toward Five Finger Falls, about 3 miles distant. Note that some of the trail signs indicate "Monte Vista Falls' which apparently is an alternate name or an older name for these same falls. Return back to this point the way you went and return back on your bicycle again along Aptos Creek Fire Road.

8.6 End of the ride back at the parking area.

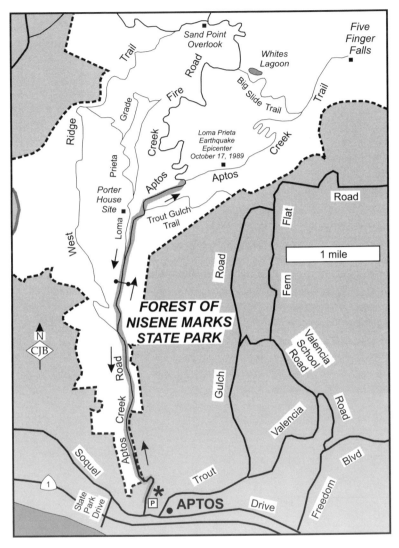

Ride No. 6

7 Aptos

Forest of Nisene Marks State Park — Sand Point Overlook

Difficulty Rating: *Moderate*	**Total Distance:** *18 miles*
Skill Level: *Non-technical*	**Off-Road Distance:** *12 miles*
Elevation Gain: *1,400 feet*	**Riding Time:** *3 hours*

About the Ride

In the early part of the twentieth century logging operations were in full swing in Santa Cruz County and particularly so on land which is now *The Forest of Nisene Marks State Park*. The Loma Prieta Lumber Company had employees living on site for both cutting the timber and for processing it into lumber. In the 1950's, the Marks family purchased the property and logging operations were halted to save the remaining redwoods. In 1963, the property was given to the State of California by the Marks children in memory of their mother, Nisene, with the stipulation that the park be operated as a semi-wilderness, without major improvements. As a result of those restrictions, there are no visitor centers or ranger stations and facilities are somewhat spare.

The route of this ride leads into the park along Aptos Creek Road. After passing through the pay station, the route continues along the fire road. There are numerous historic sites in the park, remnants of the once very busy logging operations. The first 4½ miles are along a slight uphill grade but after that, the climb gets more serious. "The Incline" is a fairly steep stretch that lasts for about 1½ miles. After that the climb continues, but at a less steep grade. The route ends at a trail junction at which the Sand Point Overlook is located. Convenient benches are provided at the point where the trees open up to reveal an inspiring panorama toward Capitola and Santa Cruz. The return back is almost all downhill.

Starting Point

To get to the starting point, take Highway 1 south from Santa Cruz. Get off in Aptos at the Seacliff Beach — Aptos exit and turn left onto State Park Drive. Turn right onto Soquel Drive and follow it under a railroad bridge, after which will be Aptos Creek Road on the left side. Park near this intersection to begin the ride.

> *Facing Page Photo:*
> *Five Finger Falls*

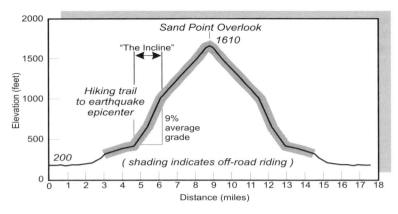

Mile Markers

- 0.0 Proceed away from Soquel Drive along Aptos Creek Road.
- 0.4 Bridge over Mangel's Creek.
- 1.2 Day use pay booth — no charge for bicycles.
- 2.1 George's Picnic Area on the right side.
- 2.2 Continue STRAIGHT over Steel Bridge.
- 3.2 Porter Family Picnic Area on the right side — continue past the gate onto Aptos Creek Fire Road.
- 3.6 The remains of the Loma Prieta Mill site is on the left side.
- 4.3 Cross bridge and begin climb up "The Incline".

Along Aptos Fire Road

9.0 Sand Point Overlook on the left side. Good spot to relax and to enjoy the view into Capitola and Santa Cruz. Return back the way you came.

18.0 End of the ride back at the parking area.

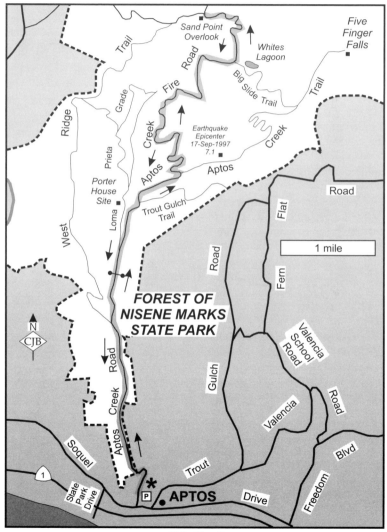

Ride No. 7

8 Soquel

Soquel Demonstration Forest

Difficulty Rating: *Difficult*	**Total Distance:** *13 miles*
Skill Level: *Very technical*	**Off-Road Distance:** *11 miles*
Elevation Gain: *1,900 feet*	**Riding Time:** *2-3 hours*

About the Ride

The California Department of Forestry operates what it calls "demonstration forests" throughout the state to show how to manage timber resources in ways that respect the natural aspects of the forests. The management methods developed make feasible the compatibility of sensible harvesting of lumber with responsible recreational usage by the general public. Located adjacent to *The Forest of Nisene Marks State Park*, the *Soquel Demonstration Forest* is one recent addition to the system, having been added in 1990.

This ride follows trails through the forest which are somewhat unique. While most state and county parks and many open space preserves prohibit bicycles from using single-track trails, the *Soquel Demonstration Forest* does not. The trails through this forest are particularly challenging, with lots of twists and turns, bumps, and steep sections to please even the most skilled mountain bikers. The legal trails throughout the forest are well-marked, so avoid using unmarked trails which can lead to private property.

The route starts at the forest entrance located on Highland Way in the heart of the Santa Cruz Mountains. It initially follows the paved road away from the forest entrance and up the hill toward the rear entrance into *The Forest of Nisene Marks State Park*. The fire road into Nisene Marks leads uphill some more before it reaches another entrance to *Soquel Demonstration Forest* at or near the top of the hill. From there the single-track begins. Narrow, winding, sometimes steep, and often overgrown, the trail leads through the forest to an overlook point with views to the west. The steep downhill sections that follow may be more safely done be lowering the saddle for added stability. At the bottom of the single-track trails, the route follows uphill along Hihn's Mill Road for the return to the starting point.

Starting Point

To get to the starting point, take Highway 17 south from Los Gatos toward Santa Cruz. At the top of the mountain get off at Summit Road and follow it back over the freeway. Continue east on Summit Road for about 4 miles and then continue another 5.5 miles after Summit Road becomes Highland Way. The forest entrance is on the right side and is easy to miss. Parking is available along the road.

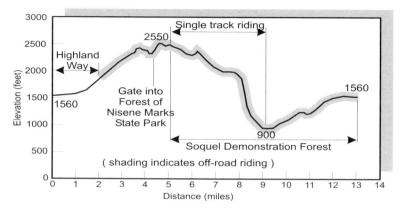

Mile Markers

0.0 Proceed SOUTH on Highland Way.

0.6 Turn Camp Loma.

2.0 Turn RIGHT onto Buzzard Lagoon Road.

2.4 Gate on the right side — private property.

2.5 Continue past the gate.

2.9 Turn RIGHT onto unmarked Aptos Creek Road (Buzzard Lagoon Road continues straight ahead).

3.5 First of several unmarked trails on the right side — do not enter.

4.3 Continue past the gate into The Forest of Nisene Marks.

5.2 Turn RIGHT off the fire road to enter Soquel Demonstration Forest on Ridge Trail. Look for an information board on the right side.

5.9 Bear LEFT to stay on Ridge Trail — Corral Trail is to the right

6.8 Turn LEFT to stay on Ridge Trail — Sulphur Springs Trail is straight ahead.

7.4 Overlook on the left side with views to the coast.

7.8 Turn RIGHT onto Tractor Trail — Ridge Trail continues straight ahead.

9.3 Turn RIGHT onto Lower Hihn's Mill Road, a wide fire road.

10.6 Continue STRAIGHT at the intersection with Sulphur Springs Trail on the right side.

13.0 Continue past the gate to exit the demonstration forest.

13.2 End of the ride at Highland Way.

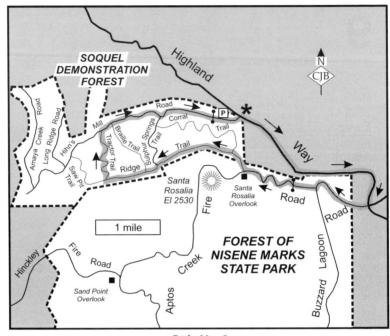

Ride No. 8

Riding the single-track in Soquel Demonstration Forest

9 Felton
Henry Cowell Redwoods State Park

Difficulty Rating: *Easy*	**Total Distance:** *6 miles*
Skill Level: *Non-technical*	**Off-Road Distance:** *5 miles*
Elevation Gain: *700 feet*	**Riding Time:** *2 hours*

About the Ride

The *Roaring Camp & Big Trees Railroad* has served for years as a fine source of family entertainment in the town of Felton, located not far from Santa Cruz. With its fully-operational steam train carrying people of all ages through the redwood forests along the old logging route, Roaring Camp has, to some extent, preserved the magic of the old days. Hikers, cyclists and equestrians enjoying the adjacent *Henry Cowell Redwoods State Park* can often hear the sound of the locomotive reverberating through the forest as it releases the pressures of its expanding steam.

While this ride is rated as an easy one, there is a substantial hill with some steep grades. Nevertheless, the ride is relatively short and on the whole it is not difficult.

The route begins in the park. The mileage markers begin at the pay station so those who choose to park outside and cycle in can set their trip cyclometers as they go past the pay station. Just past the pay station is a visitor center which has information about the park and the surrounding redwood forests. Restrooms are also provided. Near the visitor center is a short walking path leading through some of the most dramatic of the remaining redwoods. The bike route follow through the visitor center area along a paved service road, Pipeline Road. Turning off Pipeline Road onto trails, the route then climbs a short distance to a observation deck with panoramic views of the surrounding mountains and forests. The return back is along the same route that took you in.

Starting Point

To get to *Henry Cowell Redwoods State Park*, take Highway 17 toward Santa Cruz and get off at the exit for Mt. Hermon Road in Scotts Valley. Follow Mt. Hermon Road through Scotts Valley to where it ends at Graham Hill Road in Felton. Turn right onto Graham Hill Road and left onto Highway 9. The entrance to the park is about ½ mile down Highway 9 on the left side.

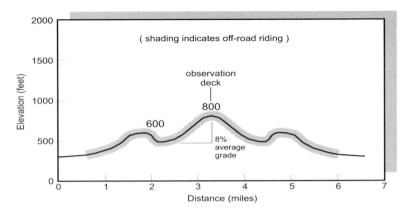

Mile Markers

0.0　Proceed into the park at the main entrance pay station located off Highway 9 just south of Felton.

0.2　Visitor center and restrooms. Look for a paved road to the rear of the restrooms. This is Pipeline Road. Turn LEFT onto Pipeline Road to head into the park.

0.8　Continue STRAIGHT as the road passes beneath the railroad tracks.

2.3　Continue STRAIGHT at the intersection with Rincon Trail on the right side and begin to climb.

2.5　Turn LEFT onto Powder Mill Trail.

3.1　Turn LEFT onto Ridge Trail toward the observation deck.

3.3　Observation deck is on the right side. This is a good place to relax and to enjoy the views from the deck. Return back the way you came on Ridge Trail.

3.5　Turn RIGHT onto Powder Mill Trail.

4.1　Turn RIGHT onto Pipeline Road.

6.4　End of the ride at the pay station.

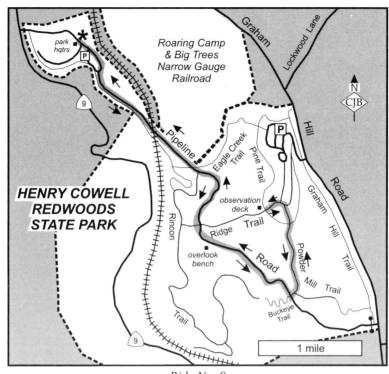

Ride No. 9

Railroad trestle across San Lorenzo River

10 Davenport
Big Basin Redwoods State Park
— Berry Creek Falls Bike & Hike

Difficulty Rating: *Easy*	**Total Bike Distance:** *12 miles*
Skill Level: *Non-technical*	**Total Hike Distance:** *3 miles*
Bike Elevation Gain: *400 feet*	**Riding Time:** *1-2 hours*
Hike Elevation Gain: *200 feet*	**Hiking Time:** *1-2 hours*

About the Ride

While the Bay Area is not particularly well-known for its abundance of waterfalls, Berry Creek Falls in *Big Basin Redwoods State Park* is an example of one that is as spectacular as any. Many people visit the falls by hiking from the main park headquarters located in the center of the Santa Cruz Mountains between Saratoga and Boulder Creek. That hike is not an easy one. Covering a distance of about 5 miles in each direction, the hike takes the better part of a day for most people. Another option is to ride a mountain bike in from a park entrance on the coast at Waddell Beach to a point from which a one-mile hike can be made.

The route to the falls is as easy to follow as can be imagined. From the trailhead at Waddell Beach, a fire road leads into the park. Generally following along Waddell Creek at first, and then along Berry Creek, the trail ends at a point beyond which bikes are not permitted. A bike rack is provided there for convenient stacking and locking. Clear trail signs indicate the way to the falls. Sturdy hiking boots or shoes should be used for the hike, since the trail can be difficult in biking shoes.

The falls are best visited in late-winter or in the springtime when the rains provide the maximum water run-off. Berry Creek Falls is only one of the falls to see. Farther upstream, less than a mile, are Silver Falls and Golden Falls Cascade. The trail along those falls is quite steep and hikers are aided by steps and a cable to provide added stability. This should not be missed.

Starting Point

Start the ride at the Waddell Beach gate into *Big Basin Redwoods State Park*, located about 19 miles north of Santa Cruz and 14 miles south of Pescadero on Highway 1.

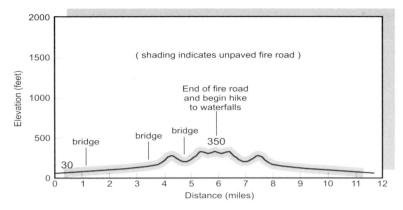

Mile Markers

0.0 Proceed past the gate into the park along the paved road.

0.4 Continue past the park office through another gate along the unpaved fire road.

1.1 Continue across a bridge.

1.8 Twin Redwoods Trail Camp on the left side.

3.4 Continue across a bridge. McCrary Ridge Trail intersection is on the right side.

4.3 Top of a small hill.

4.9 Continue across a bridge.

5.3 Top of a small hill.

5.4 Henry Creek trail intersection on the left side.

5.6 Continue across another bridge.

5.8 End of the fire road. Locate the bike rack to lock your bike and begin the hike. At the end of the hike, return the way you came.

11.6 End of the ride back at Waddell Beach.

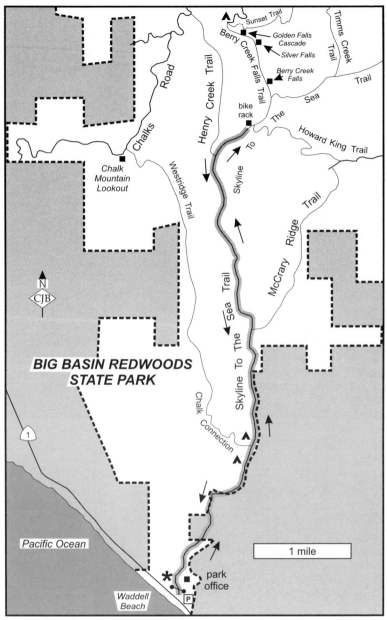

Ride No. 10

11 Saratoga
Big Basin Redwoods State Park

Difficulty Rating: *Moderate*	**Total Distance:** *16 miles*
Skill Level: *Non-technical*	**Off-Road Distance:** *11 miles*
Elevation Gain: *1,500 feet*	**Riding Time:** *2-3 hours*

About the Ride

Heavy logging of the majestic redwood trees in the Santa Cruz Mountains has taken away most of the old-growth specimens. Some remain however, and the younger second-growth trees are gradually reclaiming the forests, often growing from the stumps of the trees that were harvested earlier. Since 1902, *Big Basin Redwoods State Park* has protected a large area in the mountains from further logging and has served as a destination for people seeking recreation in the still-beautiful and lush forests.

This ride follows a route around the eastern portion of the park nearest to the visitor center and park headquarters. Starting at the visitor center, where there is an excellent display about the park, the route first leads into the park along a paved service road past picnic areas and hiking trailheads. After the passing the picnic areas, the road becomes an unpaved trail and leads uphill to Big Basin Highway, the main road to the park from Saratoga. A short distance along the road leads to more climbing along China Grade, to reach a fire road into the park at the top of a ridge. Middle Ridge Fire Road and then Johansen Road follow an exhilarating descent through the woods toward the west. The return back is along a relatively short climb up Gazos Creek Road.

Riding on fire roads and paved roads ensures that no special mountain biking skills are necessary. Substantial climbing is to be expected however, so a good physical workout will result.

Starting Point

Big Basin is located in the Santa Cruz Mountains above Saratoga. To get there, take Big Basin Way (Highway 9) through the town of Saratoga and follow it up to Skyline Boulevard at the top. Continue past Skyline Boulevard for about 6 miles and then turn right onto Highway 236 toward Big Basin. There is a small fee to enter the park and plenty of parking once inside. Begin the ride at the pay station at the entrance.

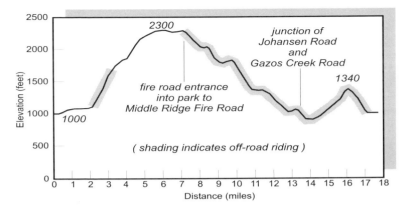

Mile Markers

0.0   Proceed into the park along the paved road. This is North Escape Road.

0.3   Continue STRAIGHT at the road intersection on the left side.

1.2   Continue past the gate as the road ends and a paved path begins.

1.4   Cross a bridge.

2.5   Cross another bridge and begin climbing.

3.6   Continue past the gate and turn LEFT onto Big Basin Highway (Highway 236.)

4.5   Turn LEFT onto China Grade.

6.9   Continue STRAIGHT at the road intersection on the right side.

7.8   Turn LEFT to go into the park on Middle Ridge Fire Road and continue past the gate.

8.6   Turn RIGHT onto Johansen Road.

11.0   At the major intersection of fire roads, turn LEFT onto Gazos Creek Road and then make another LEFT to stay on Gazos Creek Road.

13.7   At the lowest elevation point in the ride, begin climbing.

16.0   Continue STRAIGHT at the intersection with Middle Ridge Fire Road.

17.1   Turn RIGHT onto North Escape Road to head back toward the visitor center.

17.4   End of the ride at park headquarters.

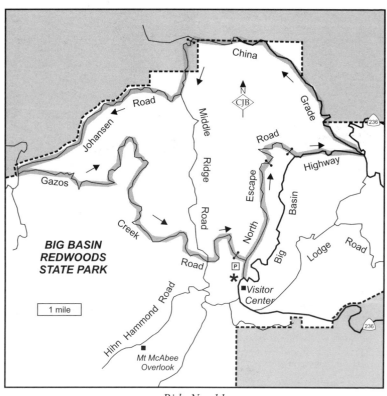

Ride No. 11

12 Santa Cruz
Wilder Ranch State Park

Difficulty Rating: *Difficult*	**Total Distance:** *13 miles*
Skill Level: *Very technical*	**Off-Road Distance:** *13 miles*
Elevation Gain: *1,600 feet*	**Riding Time:** *3 hours*

About the Ride

Single-track trails through forests and across meadows and numerous stream crossings give *Wilder Ranch State Park* a variety rarely found in mountain biking. Formerly an operating ranch, it is now a state park and cultural preserve. The ranch buildings are set up as museums and they give the visitor a sense of what life was like here in times past.

This ride leads through the park in a way intended to highlight the most interesting and challenging trails. Starting at the main parking area for the park, the route leads first through the ranch compound, crosses under Highway 1, and then heads up immediately into the hills. After a climb along a fire road, single-track trails through the dense forest lead to a very challenging single-track along Enchanted Loop. The downhill is bumpy and steep, the uphill, just steep. After the Enchanted Loop, the route then leads uphill along Eucalyptus Loop Trail to reach the highest point in the ride. A long downhill on Long Meadow Trail and then Engelsman Loop Trail brings you back to the parking area.

An additional loop from the parking lot is not included in this ride, but can be done before or after it. Leading from the parking area, Old Cove Landing Trail is an easy 3-mile loop that runs along the shoreline and then back to the parking area. Spectacular scenery, more than challenging riding, makes this loop one not to be missed.

Starting Point

Wilder Ranch is located on Highway 1, about 2 miles north of Santa Cruz. There is a modest day use fee that can be avoided by parking along the highway and biking in. The route mileage begins at the parking area.

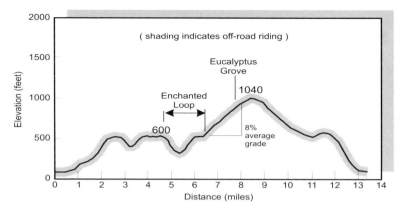
(shading indicates off-road riding)

Mile Markers

0.0 Proceed toward Santa Cruz along the paved service road.

0.1 Turn LEFT, walk your bike past the old ranch buildings, and then ride through the tunnel under the roadway.

0.4 Bear LEFT to continue around the left side of the corral.

0.5 Continue past the trail intersection on the left, cross over a bridge and then bear LEFT onto Engelsman Loop Trail.

1.9 Turn LEFT onto Wild Boar Trail.

2.4 Turn LEFT onto Old Cabin Trail.

2.7 Cross over stream on small bridge.

3.4 Turn LEFT onto Eucalyptus Loop Trail.

3.9 Cross over stream on small bridge.

4.3 Cross over another stream on small bridge.

4.4 Trail intersection on the left side.

4.7 Turn LEFT onto main fire road and into the major trail junction. There are two trails ahead indicating Enchanted Loop. Continue along the leftmost of the two trails onto Enchanted Loop.

4.9 Turn RIGHT onto the main fire road.

5.4 Turn RIGHT onto Enchanted Loop and then bear RIGHT at the trail split — Baldwin Trail is to the left.

6.6 Back at the main trail intersection — turn LEFT to head uphill along Eucalyptus Loop Trail.

7.8 Turn LEFT onto Chinquapin Trail.

8.7 Turn RIGHT onto Long Meadow Trail.

11.0 Turn LEFT onto Engelsman Loop Trail.

12.7 Cross bridge and continue STRAIGHT along the main trail toward the tunnel and the ranch buildings, retracing your route back to the main parking lot.

13.3 End of the ride at the parking area.

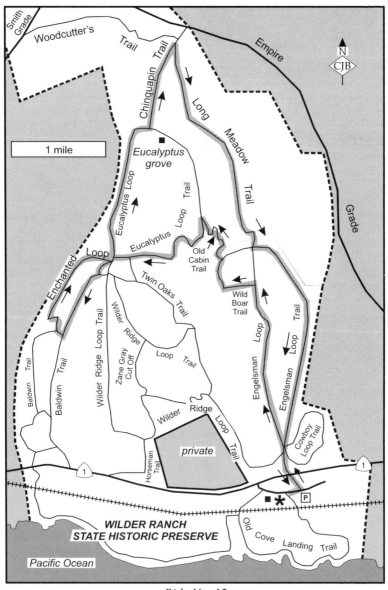

Smith Grade

Woodcutter's Trail

Empire

Chinquapin Trail

Long Meadow Trail

Grade

N
CJB

1 mile

Eucalyptus grove

Eucalyptus Loop

Loop Trail

Enchanted Loop

Eucalyptus Loop

Old Cabin Trail

Twin Oaks Trail

Wild Boar Trail

Baldwin Trail

Baldwin Trail

Wilder Ridge Loop Trail

Wilder Ridge Loop Trail

Zane Gray Cut Off

Engelsman Loop

Engelsman Loop

Wilder Ridge Loop Trail

private

Horseman Trail

Cowboy Loop Trail

1

1

P

*

WILDER RANCH
STATE HISTORIC PRESERVE

Old Cove Landing Trail

Pacific Ocean

Ride No. 12

13   Santa Cruz
Wilder Ranch State Park,
UC Santa Cruz, and Pogonip Preserve

Difficulty Rating: *Moderate*	**Total Distance:** *16 miles*
Skill Level: *Somewhat technical*	**Off-Road Distance:** *6 miles*
Elevation Gain: *1,600 feet*	**Riding Time:** *2-3 hours*

About the Ride

Most mountain biking routes take place within a single preserve or park. However, it can sometimes be more enjoyable to ride in connecting places, thereby enlarging the experience and even making it somewhat of an adventure.

This route follows along trails in *Wilder Ranch State Park*, through the lands of the *University of California at Santa Cruz* and through *Pogonip Preserve*. There is a fair amount of road riding in the route. The climbs are along the roads and the descents are generally along the trails.

The route begins in Santa Cruz at Harvey West Park, where there are restrooms and public parking. From there, the route follows surface roads uphill and past the beautiful campus of UCSC. The trails begin in *Wilder Ranch State Park*. Woodcutter's Trail is one of the least-traveled trails in the park and leads to Smith Grade for another climb on pavement. The next trails are those which lead through the undeveloped land of the UCSC campus and to the *Pogonip Preserve*, a nature area owned and administered by the City of Santa Cruz. The trail through Pogonip is short but sweet and leads to Highway 9 for the downhill return to Harvey West Park.

Most of the trails are wide fire roads but sections of Woodcutter's Trail are narrow and may be quite rutted. The trail through Pogonip is single-track with sharp switchbacks.

Starting Point

Star the ride in Santa Cruz at Harvey West Park. To get there, take Highway 17 to Santa Cruz and then Highway 1 north. Turn right onto River Street (Highway 9) toward Boulder Creek and then left onto Fern Street. Turn left onto Limekiln Street (which becomes Coral Street) and follow it to Evergreen Street. At the end of Evergreen Street is Harvey West Park.

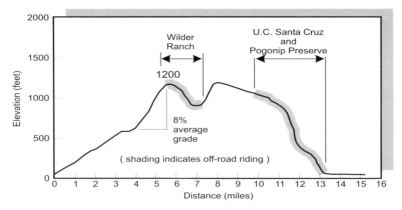

Mile Markers

0.0   Proceed out of Harvey West Park along Evergreen Street.

0.2   Turn RIGHT onto the bike path just before Evergreen Street turns sharply left.

0.4   Continue STRAIGHT onto High Street at the end of the bike path.

1.6   Continue STRAIGHT at the intersection with Bay Street on the left and Coolidge Drive on the right. Begin Empire Grade.

5.2   Turn LEFT and go past the gate onto Chinquapin Trail into Wilder Ranch State Park.

5.5   Turn RIGHT onto Woodcutter's Trail.

7.2   Turn RIGHT onto fire road at end of Woodcutter's Trail.

7.5   Turn RIGHT onto Smith Grade and climb.

8.5   Turn RIGHT onto Empire Grade.

9.9   Turn LEFT and go past the gate onto Chinquapin Road and onto the UC Santa Cruz campus.

10.6   Seven Springs Trail intersection on the right side.

11.1   Bear LEFT at the 4-way trail intersection to stay on Chinquapin Road.

12.0   Turn LEFT onto Fuel Brake Road toward Pogonip and then continue past a gate and around the right side of a communication tower.

12.3   Bear LEFT to enter Pogonip Preserve along U-Con Trail.

13.1   Turn LEFT onto Rincon Trail.

13.3   Bear RIGHT to stay on Rincon Trail and then turn RIGHT onto Highway 9 to head back to Santa Cruz.

15.5   Turn RIGHT onto Encinal Street and then LEFT onto Limekiln Street.

16.2   End of the ride at the Harvey West Park.

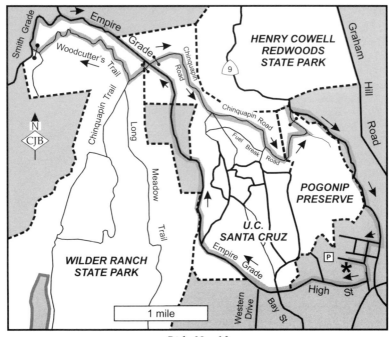

Ride No. 13

Chinquapin Trail

The San Francisco Peninsula

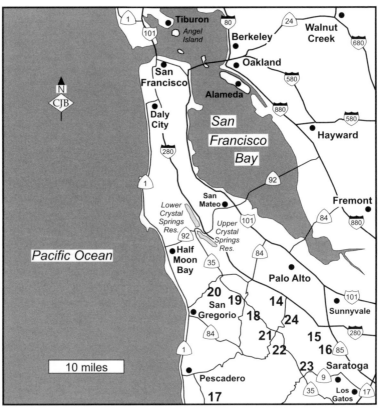

Ride 14. Palo Alto — Arastradero Preserve .... Page 55
Ride 15. Cupertino — Monte Bello........................ Page 58
Ride 16. Cupertino — Fremont Older Open Space Preserve...... Page 61
Ride 17. Pescadero — Butano State Park .... Page 64
Ride 18. Woodside — El Corte de Mader Open Space Preserve... Page 67
Ride 19. Woodside — Purisima Creek Redwoods.............. Page 70
Ride 20. Loma Mar — Old Haul Road .... Page 73
Ride 21. Palo Alto — Russian Ridge Open Space Preserve ...... Page 76
Ride 22. Palo Alto — Skyline Ridge Open Space Preserve....... Page 79
Ride 23. Saratoga — Saratoga Gap and Long Ridge Preserves.... Page 82
Ride 24. Portola Valley — Alpine Road and Windy Hill .... Page 85

14 Palo Alto
Arastradero Preserve

Difficulty Rating: *Easy*
Skill Level: *Somewhat technical*
Elevation Gain: *600 feet*

Total Distance: *5 miles*
Off-Road Distance: *5 miles*
Riding Time: *1-2 hours*

About the Ride

With its relatively small hills and with trails that alternate between single-track and fire road, and with its close proximity to Palo Alto, *Arastradero Preserve* is an ideal place for the beginner mountain bike enthusiast to practice skills and to develop endurance. Plentiful trees along Arastradero Creek and around the lake provide for welcome shade on hot summer days.

Administered by the city of Palo Alto, *Arastradero Preserve* is a popular destination for hikers, runners and equestrians, as well as cyclists. Courteous behavior is essential to making multi-use preserves work.

This easy tour of the preserve is offered as a simple introduction to mountain biking. Small hills and some narrow trails allow the beginner cyclist to develop basic riding skills without the need to tackle extended climbs. This route leads from the main parking area for the preserve along a variety of trails past the lake, along the creek, and up and down some small hills for a complete tour around the preserve.

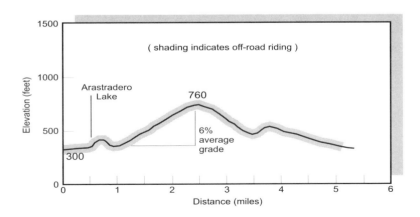

Starting Point

To get to *Arastradero Preserve*, take highway 280 to Palo Alto and get off at the exit for Page Mill Road. Head west on Page Mill Road for about ¼ mile and then turn right onto Arastradero Road. The parking area is about ½ mile down along Arastradero Road.

Mile Markers

0.0   From the parking area, proceed along Gateway Trail, the trail that goes parallel to Arastradero Road in the general direction toward Page Mill Road.

0.1   Cross the road to get into the main area of the preserve and continue along Juan Bautista de Anza Trail.

0.4   Bear LEFT at the intersection with Meadowlark Trail on the right side to stay on Juan Bautista de Anza Trail.

0.6   Arastradero Lake is on the left side. Turn LEFT and follow Paseo del Roble Trail to Lake Trail for a view of the lake. Return back and then continue along Juan Bautista de Anza Trail.

0.9   Turn LEFT just past the lake onto Arastradero Creek Trail.

1.4   Turn RIGHT onto Acorn Trail and climb a short hill.

1.8   Turn LEFT to continue on Meadowlark Trail.

2.3   Continue STRAIGHT at the intersection with Woodrat Trail on the left side and then look for the trail on the right which goes a short distance to a vista point.

2.6   Turn LEFT onto Bowl Loop.

2.9   Turn LEFT onto Bowl Loop Trail.

3.3   Turn LEFT to get back onto Meadowlark Trail.

3.4   Turn RIGHT onto Woodland Star Trail.

3.8   Turn RIGHT and then LEFT to get on Bay Laurel Trail.

3.9   Bear LEFT onto Ohlone Trail.

4.1   Turn RIGHT onto Juan Bautista de Anza Trail.

4.3   Turn LEFT to get back onto Meadowlark Trail.

4.7   Turn LEFT onto Portola Pastures Trail.

4.9   Turn RIGHT to head toward the road.

5.1   Turn RIGHT onto Arastradero Road.

5.3   End of the ride back at the parking area.

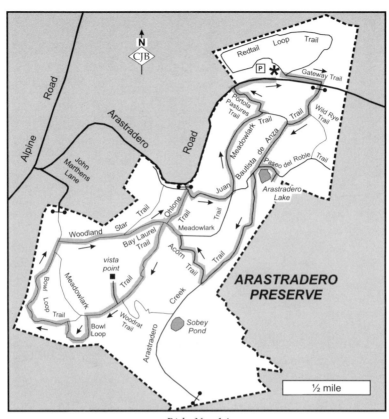

Ride No. 14
Meadowlark Trail in Arastradero Preserve

15 Cupertino
Monte Bello Open Space Preserve

Difficulty Rating: *Difficult*	**Total Distance:** *17 miles*
Skill Level: *Somewhat technical*	**Off-Road Distance:** *7 miles*
Elevation Gain: *2,500 feet*	**Riding Time:** *3-4 hours*

About the Ride

The upper Stevens Creek watershed, from the grassy slopes of Monte Bello Ridge to the brush and oak-covered woodlands below, is contained within the *Monte Bello Open Space Preserve*. Located in the Santa Cruz Mountains high above Cupertino, Monte Bello is the largest preserve managed by the Midpeninsula Regional Open Space District. While the primary access into the preserve is on Page Mill Road about one mile from Skyline Boulevard near the top of the mountain range, there are other ways to get in as well.

This ride utilizes one of those entry points. Starting well below Monte Bello at Stevens Creek Reservoir, the route leads uphill immediately along paved Montebello Road. After a long climb, the road ends and a trail leads into the preserve, climbing some more until it reaches the top of Black Mountain, the site of microwave communication towers.

After passing the communication towers, the route then descends into Stevens Canyon along Indian Creek Trail, affording stunning views of the hills and valleys which form the watershed. The descent continues along Stevens Canyon Trail and finally exits the preserve onto Stevens Canyon Road for the easy return to the start point.

Starting Point

The ride starts in Cupertino on Stevens Canyon Road just past Stevens Creek Dam. Follow Highway 280 and take the exit for Foothill Expressway and Grant Road. Note that there are several exits for Foothill Expressway, so be sure to take the one in Cupertino, not far from the Highway 85 interchange. Continue west along Foothill Boulevard and cross Stevens Creek Boulevard. Keep going as the road name changes to Stevens Canyon Road. Continue past the dam to a small parking area on the left side of the road just after the intersection with Montebello Road. Park here to begin the ride.

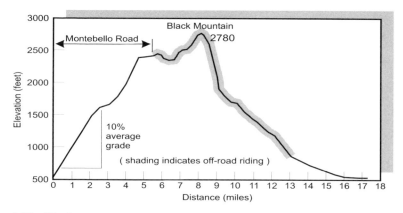

Mile Markers

0.0   Proceed EAST on Stevens Canyon Road, back toward the dam and turn LEFT onto Montebello Road. Begin climbing immediately.

5.2   Turn LEFT and pass through gate "MB08" onto Water Wheel Trail.

6.6   Turn LEFT onto Monte Bello Road (fire road).

7.8   Black Mountain summit at the microwave towers — elevation is 2,780 feet.

8.0   Turn LEFT onto Indian Creek Trail.

8.2   Continue STRAIGHT at the trail intersection on the right side.

8.8   After a long descent, turn LEFT onto Stevens Canyon Trail.

10.8   Continue STRAIGHT at the intersection with Grizzly Flat Trail on the right side.

11.2   Continue STRAIGHT at the intersection with Table Mountain Trail on the right side.

12.5   Continue past the gate onto Stevens Canyon Road.

14.4   Continue STRAIGHT at the intersection with Redwood Gulch Road on the right side.

16.1   Continue STRAIGHT at the intersection with Mt. Eden Road on the right side.

17.3   End of the ride at the parking area.

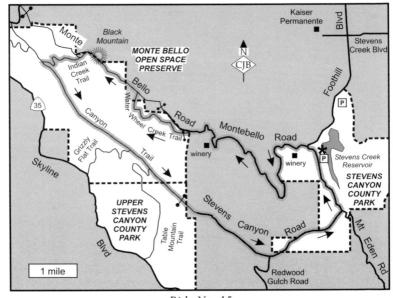

Ride No. 15

Waterwheel Trail in Monte Bello

16 Cupertino
Fremont Older Open Space Preserve

Difficulty Rating: *Moderate*	**Total Distance:** *6 miles*
Skill Level: *Somewhat technical*	**Off-Road Distance:** *6 miles*
Elevation Gain: *1,300 feet*	**Riding Time:** *1-2 hours*

About the Ride

Contemporary living in the fast-paced Silicon Valley often leaves little time for recreational pursuits. Most of the best mountain biking areas are located too distant to permit a quick after-work ride. *Fremont Older Open Space Preserve* is a pleasant exception. Located in the foothills near Cupertino, it offers plenty of challenge and yet is easily accessible.

This route through Fremont Older begins at the trailhead located at the end of Prospect Road. The trail requires a climb initially along a single-track section and then along wide fire roads and more single-track to get to Hunter's Point with a broad view into the valley below. More up-and-down trails and fire roads lead to the far end of the preserve and then return back to the start point.

The trails are well-marked and cyclists need to observe courtesy in sharing the trails with hikers, runners and equestrians. Poison oak is present, as it is within most of the preserves in the Santa Cruz Mountains.

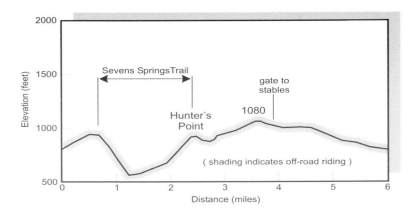

Starting Point

To get to the trailhead, take Highway 85 toward Cupertino and get off at the exit for De Anza Boulevard. Follow De Anza Boulevard toward Saratoga and turn right after a short distance onto Prospect Road. After 0.4 miles, turn left to stay on Prospect Road. At the very end of Prospect Road is the trailhead. The parking is limited at the trailhead, so it may be necessary to park further down the road and to bike in.

Mile Markers

0.0   From the parking area, take the Cora Older Trail and proceed to climb along single-track. Bikes are not permitted on the fire road at this point.

0.4   Turn RIGHT onto the main fire road.

0.5   Turn RIGHT onto Seven Springs Trail.

1.2   At the bottom, continue STRAIGHT across Ranch Road to continue on Seven Springs Trail, which circles around the hill as it climbs.

2.0   At the trail intersection, continue STRAIGHT.

2.2   Turn RIGHT for the side trip steeply up to Hunter's Point, an overlook into the valley below.

2.4   After viewing Hunter's Point, go back down the short hill and turn Right onto Hayfield Trail.

2.5   Continue STRAIGHT at a trail intersection on the right side.

2.6   Bear RIGHT at a trail split to continue on Hayfield Trail.

2.9   Bear RIGHT at the intersection with Toyon Trail on the left side.

3.1   Turn LEFT onto Coyote Ridge Trail.

3.2   Bear LEFT to stay on Coyote Ridge Trail — Lookout Trail goes to the right.

3.3   Bear RIGHT to stay on Coyote Ridge Trail.

3.5   Maisie's Peak — continue STRAIGHT ahead.

3.9   Continue STRAIGHT through the opening in the fence. Garrod Farms gate is on the right side. Continue around the left side of the water tank.

4.2   Turn LEFT onto Toyon Trail.

4.8   Bear RIGHT to stay on Toyon Trail.

5.2   Bear RIGHT again to stay on Toyon Trail.

5.5   Turn RIGHT to get back onto Hayfield Trail, the main fire road you came in on.

5.8   Turn RIGHT to head toward Prospect Road.

5.9   Turn LEFT onto Cora Older Trail.

6.3   End of the ride at the parking area.

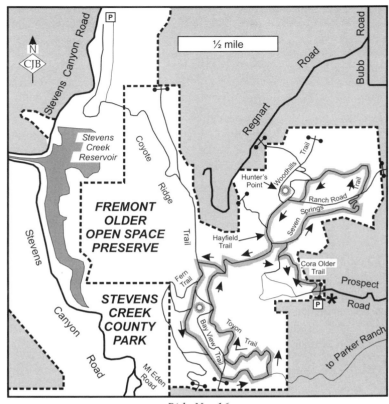

Ride No. 16

Equestrians in Fremont Older Preserve

17   **Pescadero**
Butano State Park

Difficulty Rating: *Moderate*	**Total Distance:** *12 miles*
Skill Level: *Somewhat technical*	**Off-Road Distance:** *10 miles*
Elevation Gain: *2,000 feet*	**Riding Time:** *2-3 hours*

About the Ride

Just south of the tiny community of Pescadero lies *Butano State Park* (locally pronounced bū'tan-o). The name, Butano, was originally shown on early maps of the area as "Beutno," from the Ohlone Indian language, meaning "friendly meeting place." The popular, and corrupted, pronunciation (bū-tan'o) is actually Spanish for "butane."

Somewhat isolated from most Bay Area cities, yet only one hour south of San Francisco on Highway 1, Butano has retained its charm as a quiet getaway for campers and hikers, as well as for mountain bike enthusiasts. Once the home of indigenous Ohlone Indians, and later of settlers who logged the lush mountains heavily, it now is undergoing a constant recovery as the second-growth redwoods regain the majesty of their ancestors. While most trails inside the park are off-limits to bicycles, fire roads around the park periphery permit mountain bikers to experience the beauty of the mountains from the ridges above.

The route of this ride first follows Cloverdale Road from the park entrance north about a mile to a trailhead for Butano Fire Road. The climb along the ridge is on a fairly gentle grade, as the fire road gradually rises above the park valley and ultimately crosses an old landing strip. Views both to the east and to the coast in the west from the ridge top present themselves at the top of the climb. The return back to the park center is along Olmo Fire Road, a route that is generally downhill, but that also has some steep uphill sections along the way.

The main climb along Butano Fire Road is long but not steep. The trails are all wide and not technical. The only steep uphill sections are along the descent on Olmo Fire Road.

Starting Point

Start the ride at the entrance to *Butano State Park*. From Palo Alto, head west on Page Mill Road and follow it all the way to Skyline Boulevard at the top. Continue straight across Skyline Boulevard to get on Alpine Road and proceed toward Pescadero. Turn left on Pescadero Road at the bottom of the hill. Go over another hill and then, just before entering Pescadero, turn left onto Cloverdale Road. *Butano State Park* is on Cloverdale Road, about 4 miles distant.

To get there from Santa Cruz, go north along Highway 1. Continue for about 19 miles and then turn right onto Gazos Creek Road. Turn left onto Cloverdale Road and the park entrance is about 1 mile away.

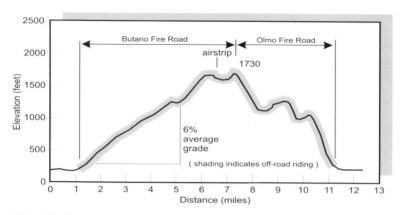

Mile Markers

0.0   Proceed NORTH along Cloverdale Road.

0.9   Look for the fire road on the right side before you get to Canyon Road. Turn RIGHT onto the fire road — Butano Fire Road — and proceed around the gate which is usually locked.

2.5   Mill Ox Trail intersection on the right side.

3.6   Bear RIGHT at the trail split. To the left is private property.

4.1   Pass through an unused open gate.

4.3   Continue STRAIGHT on Butano Fire Road at the intersection with Jackson Flats Trail on the right side.

6.2   Continue STRAIGHT across an abandoned airstrip.

6.7   Continue STRAIGHT on Butano Fire Road at the intersection with the trail to the Butano Trail Camp on the right side.

7.1   Turn RIGHT onto Olmo Fire Road. This is EASY TO MISS. If you reach the trailhead for the Ray Linder Memorial Trail on the left side, you went too far.

8.1   Indian Trail intersection on the right side.

8.8   There is a short trail on the left side to an overlook with a bench.

9.9   Goat Hill Trail intersection on the right side.

10.4 Año Nuevo Trail intersection on the left side.

11.0 Turn LEFT onto the service road at the end of the Olmo Fire Road.

11.6 Turn LEFT on the main paved road toward the park exit.

12.4 Back at the start point.

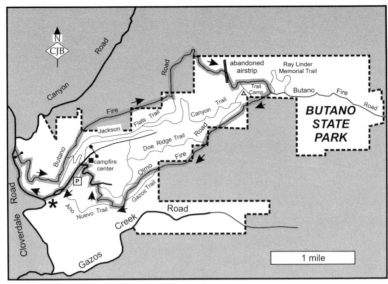

Ride No.17

View into Butano State Park

18 Woodside
El Corte de Madera Open Space Preserve

Difficulty Rating: *Difficult*	**Total Distance:** *10 miles*
Skill Level: *Very technical*	**Off-Road Distance:** *10 miles*
Elevation Gain: *2,200 feet*	**Riding Time:** *2-3 hours*

About the Ride

Car drivers cruising on a weekend morning along Skyline Boulevard above Woodside must wonder what is going on when they drive past Skegg's Point overlook. This is the time of peak activity for mountain bikers as the parking area is usually crowded with bikes and sometimes resembles a staging area for a bike race. Just across the road from Skegg's Point lies one of the most popular mountain bike destinations for advanced cyclists looking to improve their skills or simply to enjoy the challenges of the terrain in *El Corte de Madera Open Space Preserve*. The location of El Corte de Madera on the steep western slope of the Santa Cruz Mountains is what causes the trails to be so challenging. Bumpy, narrow and steep, the trails here are some of the most difficult around.

This ride follows a route through El Corte de Madera along some of its most popular trails. Single-track trails through thick forests and along constantly changing slopes provide both challenge and visual delights. Leading first along El Corte de Madera Creek Trail, the route descends and then crosses the creek. More gnarly sections along Resolution Trail and Fir Trail lead to a view point which serves as a good spot to rest and to catch your breath. Shortly after continuing, the route then leads to the Sandstone Formation, an unusual rock formation worth a side trip on foot. Manzanita, Timberview, and Crosscut Trails then lead to another place to stop. The old-growth Methuselah Tree is an example of what is not found much in the Santa Cruz Mountains — a redwood that somehow escaped the loggers. Looking to be in the neighborhood of 1,000 years old, the Methuselah Tree can be reached with a short walk down a well-marked path. Back on your bike, a fun-filled ride down Giant Salamander Trail is followed by a grunt of a climb back out of the preserve along Methuselah Trail.

The trails are mostly along narrow single-track. Steep terrain and often bumpy conditions make this one for skilled riders. Helmets are mandatory.

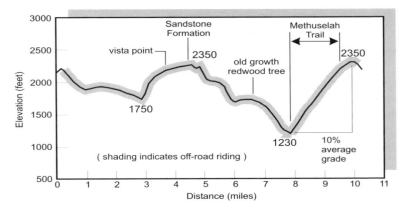

Starting Point

Start the ride at Skegg's Point overlook, located on Skyline Boulevard above Woodside. To get there from Woodside, head up Highway 84 out of Woodside and then turn right onto Kings Mountain Road. At the top, turn left on Skyline Boulevard and go about 2 miles to get to the overlook on the left side.

Mile Markers

0.0   Proceed NORTH out of the overlook parking area along the Skyline Boulevard and then turn LEFT into the preserve through gate number CM01. Continue STRAIGHT on the main trail.

0.2   Turn RIGHT onto El Corte de Madera Creek Trail.

0.9   Turn LEFT and cross over creek to stay on El Corte de Madera Creek Trail.

1.8   Bear RIGHT at the trail intersection with Tafoni Trail to stay on El Corte de Madera Creek Trail.

2.5   Turn LEFT onto Resolution Trail.

3.6   Turn LEFT onto Fir Trail.

3.7   Turn LEFT to the vista point for a view toward the west. Return from the vista point and get back on the Fir Trail to continue.

4.1   Turn LEFT onto the Tafoni Trail to see the Sandstone Formation which is about 0.1 miles up Tafoni Trail. Return from there and continue on the Fir Trail.

4.5   Turn RIGHT onto an unnamed trail to head toward Methuselah Trail.

4.6   Continue STRAIGHT at the intersection with Methuselah Trail to get onto Manzanita Trail.

5.8   Turn LEFT onto Timberview Trail.

6.0   Turn RIGHT onto Crosscut Trail.

6.1   Bear RIGHT to stay on Crosscut Trail.

6.5   Turn LEFT onto Timberview Trail.

6.7   Trail to the Methuselah Tree on the left side.

6.9   Turn RIGHT onto Giant Salamander Trail.

7.8   Turn RIGHT onto Methuselah Trail and begin steady climb out of the preserve.

9.5   Turn LEFT onto Fir Trail.

9.6   Turn RIGHT to stay on Fir Trail.

10.2   Turn RIGHT to get out of the preserve and onto Skyline Boulevard.

10.3   Back at the start point.

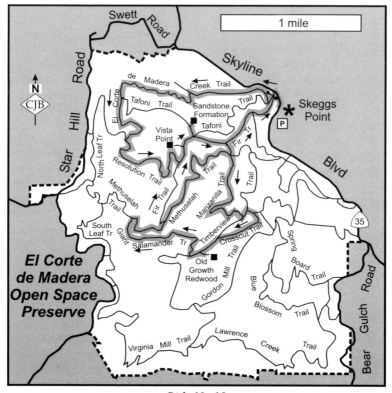

Ride No.18

19 Woodside

Purisima Creek Redwoods Open Space Preserve

Difficulty Rating: *Difficult*	**Total Distance:** *9 miles*
Skill Level: *Very technical*	**Off-Road Distance:** *7 miles*
Elevation Gain: *1,600 feet*	**Riding Time:** *2-3 hours*

About the Ride

The headwaters of the Purisima Creek form in the upper reaches of the Santa Cruz Mountains on the western slope. Following a path through lush redwood forests, the creek winds its way to the ocean at a point about 4 miles south of Half Moon Bay. The *Purisima Creek Open Space Preserve* consists of about 2,500 acres of public land open for the use of hikers, runners, equestrians and cyclists.

This ride follows a route around the preserve near its periphery and offers cyclists the full experience of the variety of terrain available there. The ride begins with a steady descent through the redwood forest along Whittemore Gulch Trail, a delightful single-track with moderate steepness. The return back up to Skyline Boulevard initially follows along a fairly flat route along the Purisima Creek Trail with numerous stream crossings over bridges. The trail then gets considerably steeper as it leads away from the creek. At the top of the climb, the route follows Skyline Boulevard the last two miles for the return back to the starting point.

Some rather steep sections of Purisima Creek Trail may require walking. Whittemore Gulch Trail is subject to seasonal closing during the wet winter months. In this case, the route can be changed by simply following Harkins Ridge Trail, an alternate way down the mountain.

Starting Point

Begin the ride at the main parking area for *Purisima Creek Redwoods*. To get there, take Highway 280 to Woodside and get off at the exit for Woodside Road (Highway 84). Follow Woodside Road west and through the center of Woodside and then turn right onto Kings Mountain Road. Follow Kings Mountain Road to the top of the mountains and turn right on Skyline Boulevard. The parking area is on the left side, about 2½ miles distant.

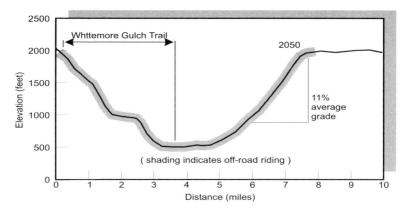

Mile Markers

0.0   Proceed into the preserve at the main trailhead on the left side of the restrooms in the parking area at gate "PC01".

0.3   Continue STRAIGHT ahead onto North Ridge Trail at the intersection with Harkins Ridge Trail on the left side.

0.8   Turn LEFT onto Whittemore Gulch Trail and begin descent with numerous switchbacks.

2.6   Cross a bridge.

3.6   Bear RIGHT at the bottom of the hill to cross over bridge and then turn LEFT onto Purisima Creek Trail.

4.6   Borden Hatch Mill Trail intersection on the right side.

4.8   Cross a bridge.

5.1   Cross another bridge.

5.4   Cross another bridge.

6.0   Soda Gulch Trail intersection on the left side.

7.9   Pass through the gate and turn LEFT onto Skyline Boulevard.

10.0   End of the ride at the main parking area.

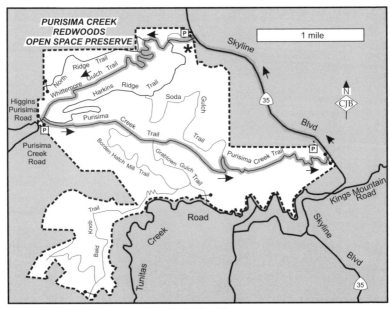

PURISIMA CREEK
REDWOODS
OPEN SPACE PRESERVE

Skyline

1 mile

North Ridge Trail

Whittemore Gulch Trail

Harkins Ridge Trail

Soda Gulch

Gulch Trail

Higgins
Purisima
Road

Purisima Creek Trail

Purisima
Creek
Road

Borden Hatch Mill Trail

Grabtown Gulch Trail

Purisima Creek Trail

Kings Mountain Road

Knob Trail

Bald

Tunitas

Creek

Road

Skyline

Blvd

N
CJB

35

35

35

Blvd

Ride No.19

Looking toward the coast from Purisima Creek Redwoods Preserve

20 Loma Mar
Old Haul Road

Difficulty Rating: *Easy*	**Total Distance:** *16 miles*
Skill Level: *Non-technical*	**Off-Road Distance:** *12 miles*
Elevation Gain: *800 feet*	**Riding Time:** *2 hours*

About the Ride

The demand for lumber created by the California gold rush in 1849 and later by the near total destruction of San Francisco in the 1906 earthquake was met by logging the seemingly endless redwood forests of the Santa Cruz Mountains. Getting the timber out of the forests required the construction of extensive roads and railroads. One of these, no longer used for logging, is today called Old Haul Road and is located within *Pescadero Creek County Park*. It follows a route through the park from the tiny hamlet of Loma Mar, located just east of Pescadero, to *Portola State Park*. Because it was formerly used as a railroad route, the grade is generally not steep and can be negotiated easily by beginner mountain bike enthusiasts.

The route of this ride begins in Loma Mar on Highway 84 and goes through *Pescadero Creek County Park* all the way to park headquarters for *Portola State Park*, a good place to walk around and have a snack. The return is back along the same route, mostly downhill.

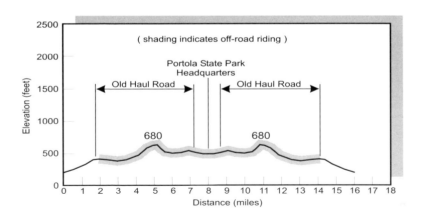

Starting Point

Start the ride in Loma Mar, about 6 miles east of Pescadero at or near the Loma Mar Store. To get there, take the Woodside Road (Highway 84) exit from Highway 280. Proceed west on Woodside Road through Woodside and over the hill toward La Honda. Just past La Honda, turn left onto Pescadero Road and follow it to Loma Mar. Park nearby and begin the mileage near the store.

Mile Markers

0.0   Proceed EAST along Pescadero Road and turn RIGHT onto Wurr Road.

1.6   Turn RIGHT into Pescadero Creek County Park on Old Haul Road and continue past the gate onto the dirt trail.

2.2   Continue past another gate.

2.4   Pomponio Trail intersection on the left side.

3.0   Towne Trail intersection on the left side.

3.5   Butano Ridge Loop Trail intersection on the right side.

5.9   Bridge Trail intersection on the left side.

6.0   Butano Ridge Loop Trail intersection on the right side.

7.1   Turn LEFT off of Old Haul Road into Portola State Park and begin a steep descent.

8.0   Portola State Park headquarters on the left side. Return back the way you came.

8.9   Turn RIGHT onto Old Haul Road, heading back toward Loma Mar.

14.4   At the end of the trail, turn RIGHT onto Wurr Road.

14.6   Turn LEFT onto Pescadero Road.

16.3   End of the ride at the Loma Mar Store.

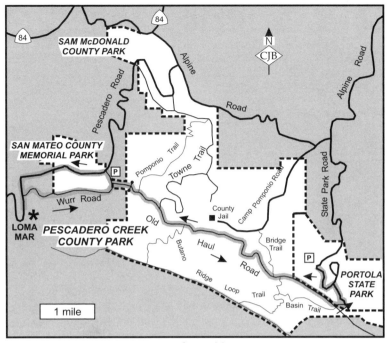

Ride No.20

Courtesy of Santa Cruz Mountains Natural History Association

IVERSON CABIN

21 Palo Alto
Russian Ridge Open Space Preserve

Difficulty Rating: *Moderate*	**Total Distance:** *11 miles*
Skill Level: *Somewhat technical*	**Off-Road Distance:** *10 miles*
Elevation Gain: *1,300 feet*	**Riding Time:** *2-3 hours*

About the Ride

At the top of the Santa Cruz Mountains, at the intersection of Skyline Boulevard and Page Mill Road, lie four separate open space preserves — *Russian Ridge, Coal Creek, Monte Bello* and *Skyline Ridge* — which are all administered by the Midpeninsula Regional Open Space District. When considered in total, the area of the four preserves forms one of the largest places in the Bay Area where cyclists, hikers and equestrians can sample the pleasures of the outdoors. A special benefit is that the preserves are already located at the mountain top, so extensive climbing is not needed to get there. The panoramic views come without the heavy price of a long climb.

This ride tours both Russian Ridge and Coal Creek and covers about 11 miles of trails through mountain meadows and coastal forests. Substantial climbing is required, as the trails follow along rolling mountain ridges for most of the route. Whereas wide fire trails predominate in Russian Ridge, Coal Creek presents some challenges associated with narrow single-track. About 1 mile along Skyline Boulevard is necessary to make the connection between the two preserves.

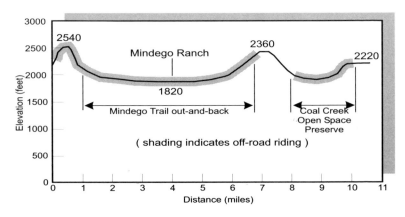

Starting Point

Start the ride at the parking lot for *Russian Ridge Open Space Preserve*. To get there, take Highway 280 to Palo Alto and get off at the exit for Page Mill Road. Follow Page Mill Road west all the way to the top at Skyline Boulevard. Cross Skyline Boulevard and go into the parking lot on the right side.

Mile Markers

0.0   Proceed NORTH out of the parking lot on Ridge Trail, heading toward Borel Hill.

0.6   Bear RIGHT to stay on Ridge Trail.

0.8   Bear LEFT to stay on Ridge Trail — Borel Hill is to the right.

1.5   Turn LEFT and LEFT again to get on Mindego Ridge Trail.

1.8   Alder Spring Trail intersection on the right side.

3.3   Turn RIGHT on the fire road to stay on Mindego Ridge Trail.

4.4   Turn AROUND at the end of the trail at Mindego Ranch and return along Mindego Ridge Trail.

5.5   Turn LEFT to continue returning along Mindego Ridge Trail.

7.1   Continue STRAIGHT at the intersection with Ridge Trail to get to Skyline Boulevard and the turn LEFT onto Skyline Boulevard.

7.8   Turn RIGHT onto unmarked and easy-to-miss Crazy Pete's Road. This road can be found by looking for the sign as you turn onto the road indicating Coal Creel Preserve.

8.1   Begin gravel road and pass through gate marked "CC06". Then enter Coal Creek at the gate marked "CC04". Turn RIGHT immediately after the gate to stay on Crazy Pete's Road toward Alpine Road.

8.4   Bear RIGHT at the intersection with Valley View Trail on the left to stay on Crazy Pete's Road.

9.2   Turn RIGHT to stay on Crazy Pete's Road.

9.5   Turn RIGHT after the barrier onto Alpine Road.

10.7   Turn RIGHT after the barrier onto Page Mill Road.

11.2   Cross Skyline Boulevard.

11.3   End of the ride at the parking area.

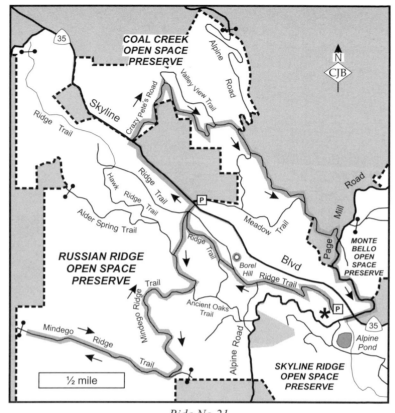

COAL CREEK OPEN SPACE PRESERVE

Skyline Ridge Trail

Alpine Road

Valley View Trail

Crazy Pete's Road

Ridge Trail

Hawk Ridge Trail

Alder Spring Trail

Meadow Trail

Page Mill Road

RUSSIAN RIDGE OPEN SPACE PRESERVE

Ridge Trail

Borel Hill

Ridge Trail

Blvd

MONTE BELLO OPEN SPACE PRESERVE

Mindego Ridge Trail

Ancient Oaks Trail

Alpine Road

Mindego Ridge Trail

SKYLINE RIDGE OPEN SPACE PRESERVE

Alpine Pond

N CJB

35

½ mile

Ride No.21

Along Mindego Ridge Trail

22 Palo Alto
Skyline Ridge Open Space Preserve

Difficulty Rating: *Moderate*	**Total Distance:** *7 miles*
Skill Level: *Somewhat-technical*	**Off-Road Distance:** *6 miles*
Elevation Gain: *1,200 feet*	**Riding Time:** *2 hours*

About the Ride

Skyline Ridge Open Space Preserve and the upper portion of *Monte Bello Open Space Preserve* are the areas covered by this ride. Located high in the Santa Cruz Mountains above Palo Alto, these preserves are just a portion of the land administered by the Midpeninsula Regional Open Space District.

The route actually begins in the parking lot for yet another preserve, Russian Ridge, located just across Alpine Road from Skyline Ridge. It leads across Alpine Road and immediately past a small pond and then up a hill into Skyline Ridge. Panoramic views into Monte Bello at the top of the hill are followed by a descent toward Horseshoe Lake. After passing the lake the route continues through the parking area for Skyline Ridge and then across Skyline Boulevard into Monte Bello. The trail through Monte Bello takes you down into the canyon which forms the watershed for Stevens Creek. Canyon Trail leads back up the hill and then some single-track leads through meadows back to Skyline Boulevard and the return to the start point.

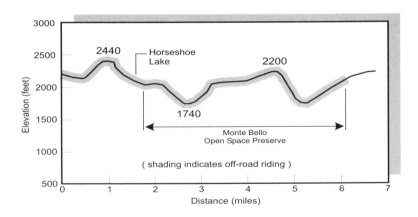

Starting Point

Start the ride at the parking lot for *Russian Ridge Open Space Preserve*. To get there, take Highway 280 to Palo Alto and get off at the exit for Page Mill Road. Follow Page Mill Road west all the way to the top at Skyline Boulevard. Cross Skyline Boulevard and go into the parking lot on the right side.

Mile Markers

0.0   Cross Alpine Road to get to the trailhead into Skyline Ridge.

0.1   Continue past the barrier to get on Alternate Ridge Trail toward Horseshoe Lake.

0.2   At Alpine Pond, bear RIGHT to stay on the bicycle-only trail around the lake and then turn LEFT on the paved road.

0.4   Dirt trail begins just after private residences.

0.6   Turn LEFT to stay on Alternate Ridge Trail.

1.0   Continue STRAIGHT at the major trail intersection.

1.4   Horseshoe Lake on the right side.

1.5   Continue past the gate and through the equestrian parking lot and turn LEFT onto the trail leading to the main parking area

1.7   Just past the main parking area, turn LEFT and cross Skyline Boulevard to reach the trailhead into Monte Bello. Just past the gate (gate "MB06"), bear LEFT and follow the trail as it runs parallel to the road

2.1   Continue STRAIGHT at the trail intersection on the left.

2.3   Continue STRAIGHT toward Canyon Trail at another trail intersection on the left side.

2.9   Turn LEFT onto Canyon Trail and begin climb toward Page Mill Road.

3.6   Trail intersection on the left.

3.8   Turn LEFT just before the gate and follow this trail parallel to the road.

4.0   Continue through the parking lot for Monte Bello along the trail running parallel to the road.

4.5   Bear LEFT at the trail split toward Skyline Boulevard.

5.5   Turn RIGHT at the end of the trail and continue toward Skyline Boulevard.

5.9   Exit Monte Bello and turn RIGHT onto Skyline Boulevard.

6.6   End of the ride at the parking area for Russian Ridge.

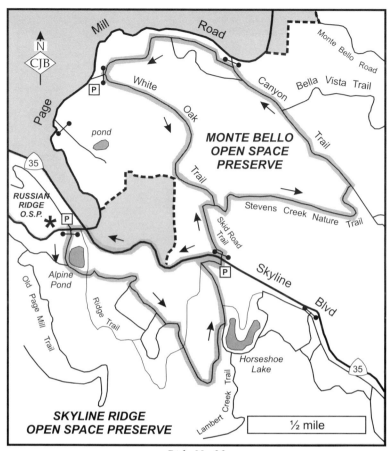

Ride No.22

The Stevens Creek Watershed, as seen from Skyline Ridge

23   Saratoga
Saratoga Gap and Long Ridge Preserves

Difficulty Rating: *Moderate*	**Total Distance:** *10 miles*
Skill Level: *Somewhat technical*	**Off-Road Distance:** *10 miles*
Elevation Gain: *900 feet*	**Riding Time:** *2 hours*

About the Ride

At the top of the mountains above Saratoga lie the *Saratoga Gap* and *Long Ridge Open Space Preserves* and *Upper Stevens Creek County Park*. The areas are adjacent and contain numerous mountain biking trails with great variety and spectacular views.

The trailhead into Saratoga Gap is the start point for this ride. It is located near the intersection of Skyline Boulevard (Highway 35) and Congress Springs Road (Highway 9). The route leads through *Saratoga Gap* along a narrow single-track through dense forest for about 2 miles to reach its end at Skyline Boulevard. This section has some steep drop-offs and is often busy with cyclists, so extra caution is advised.

After crossing Skyline Boulevard, the route leads into Long Ridge. Open meadows with expansive views to the west are interspersed with heavy forests. Narrow single-track and fire roads alternate along this route as it leads to the northernmost section of the preserve. A narrow trail then descends with sharp switchbacks to Peters Creek. Lush with ferns and cool on the hottest of days, Peters Creek Trail leads along the creek to a small pond and the climb back up to the main fire road. The return to Saratoga Gap is along the same route which brought you out there.

While the route is relatively short and the elevation gains are modest, the trails are quite narrow in places and frequently have steep drop-offs on the sides.

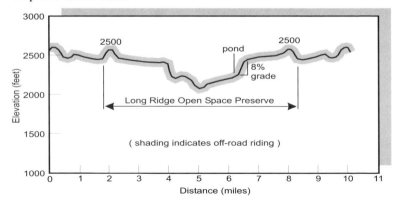

Starting Point

Start the ride at the trailhead into *Saratoga Gap Open Space Preserve*. To get there, take Highway 280 to Saratoga and get off at the exit for Saratoga Avenue. Head west on Saratoga Avenue and continue through Saratoga along Big Basin Way (Highway 9). Big Basin Way becomes Congress Springs Road and leads to Skyline Boulevard at the top, where the trailhead is located on the right side.

Mile Markers

0.0 Proceed past the gate into Saratoga Gap Open Space Preserve along Saratoga Gap Trail.

1.7 Continue STRAIGHT across dirt road.

2.0 Continue STRAIGHT across Skyline Boulevard into Long Ridge Preserve.

2.1 Turn RIGHT onto the main fire road.

2.3 Bear LEFT at the trail split and follow single-track across the meadow and through the woods.

2.5 Turn LEFT to get back on the fire road.

3.1 Bear RIGHT at the trail split to follow Ridge Trail — Ward Road is to the left.

3.3 Turn LEFT onto wide fire road — Ward Road — toward Long Ridge Road.

3.4 Continue STRAIGHT onto Long Ridge Road — Ward Road continues to the left.

3.9 Turn RIGHT toward Peters Creek Trail — gate out of the preserve is straight ahead.

4.9 Continue STRAIGHT at the trail intersection on the right — Peters Creek Loop.

5.4 Continue STRAIGHT onto Peters Creek Trail. Grizzly Flat parking area is to the left

5.8 Turn LEFT on the fire road toward Long Ridge Road.

6.4 Turn RIGHT, cross over bridge and climb along narrow trail with switchbacks.

6.9 Turn LEFT at the top of the climb onto Ward Road.

7.0 Turn RIGHT onto single-track trail.

7.2 Turn LEFT onto fire road.

7.8 Turn RIGHT onto single-track trail.

8.0 Turn RIGHT onto fire road.

8.2 Continue across Skyline Boulevard and back to the start point.

10.2 End of the ride at the trailhead for Saratoga Gap.

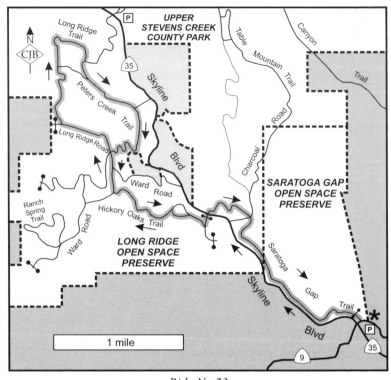

Ride No.23

Long Ridge Open Space Preserve

24 Portola Valley
Alpine Road and Windy Hill

Difficulty Rating: *Difficult*	**Total Distance:** *18 miles*
Skill Level: *Somewhat technical*	**Off-Road Distance:** *6 miles*
Elevation Gain: *2,200 feet*	**Riding Time:** *3 hours*

About the Ride

The Alpine Inn — fondly remembered by the locals as "Rossotti's" — serves as the start point for this ride. Alternating on pavement and dirt, the route leads through three open space preserves and offers views from the top in all directions. Initially going through rural Portola Valley along and to the end of Alpine Road, the route then continues on the old section of Alpine Road, a fire road which leads up the hill to Page Mill Road, near the top of the Santa Cruz Mountains. At the end of the climb along the dirt road, a short stretch on Page Mill Road leads to *Russian Ridge Open Space Preserve* and a brief pass through on some single-track to the highest point in the ride. A 4-mile jaunt back on the pavement along Skyline Boulevard leads to *Windy Hill Open Space Preserve*. In Windy Hill, there is only one trail legal for bikes, Spring Ridge Trail, and that trail leads downhill quickly to Portola Road and the return to Alpine Inn.

The main climb in the route is along the dirt fire road section of old Alpine Road. *As of this writing, there is a section of the fire road about 1 mile up on the dirt part of Alpine Road (at the 5.5 mile point in the route) that is temporarily washed out.* There is no safe way to get directly through along Alpine Road. However, there are some makeshift trails leading around the washout and back onto Alpine Road. The route directions below do *not* include the bypass around the washout.

Single-track trails along the ridge through Russian Ridge will keep you alert while the long downhill through Windy Hill will require constant application of the brakes. For the most part, the paved roads along the route have wide bicycle lanes and car traffic that is usually very courteous toward bicycles.

Starting Point

The ride starts in Portola Valley at the intersection of Alpine Road and Arastradero Road. To get there, take Highway 280 to Portola Valley and get off at the exit for Alpine Road. Follow Alpine Road west for about a mile to the intersection with Arastradero Road. It is usually acceptable to park in the big parking area at Alpine Inn. Be sure to park away from the restaurant so that its business is not impacted by your presence there.

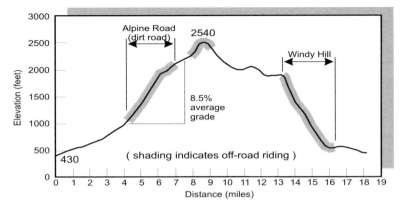

Mile Markers

0.0   Proceed WEST along Alpine Road, heading toward the hills.

1.1   Continue STRAIGHT at the intersection with Portola Road.

4.5   Turn RIGHT off the paved road to begin the fire road. You will recognize this point by the steep hill ahead of you through the portals on the paved road and by the gate off the road on the right marking the entry to the fire road.

7.1   Turn RIGHT onto Page Mill Road.

7.8   Cross over Skyline Boulevard and then turn RIGHT into the parking area for Russian Ridge. Proceed on the Ridge Trail at the far end of the parking area.

8.4   Bear RIGHT to stay on Ridge Trail.

8.6   Bear LEFT to stay on Ridge Trail — Borel Hill is to the right.

9.3   Turn LEFT and the RIGHT to get to Skyline Boulevard. Turn LEFT on Skyline Boulevard

11.7   The first gate into Windy Hill is on the right side — bikes are not permitted on this trail.

12.5   Second entrance for Windy Hill on the right side.

13.1   Main entrance for Windy Hill on the right side.

13.5   Turn RIGHT into Windy Hill at gate "WH01". Follow the Spring Ridge Trail all the way to Portola Road.

16.1   Continue past the gate and turn RIGHT onto gravel road and then RIGHT onto Portola Road.

17.1   Turn LEFT onto Alpine Road.

18.2   End of the ride at the Alpine Inn.

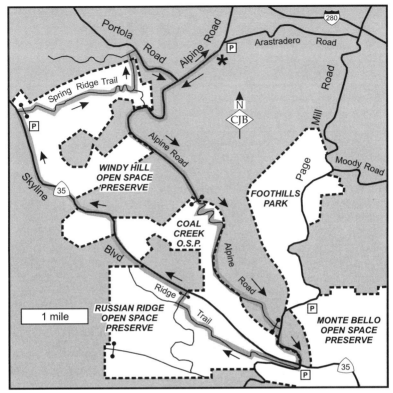

Ride No.24

View from Russia Ridge

The East Bay

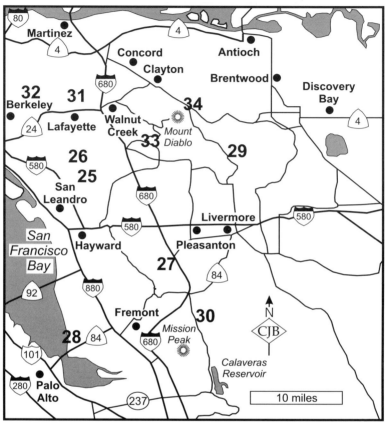

Ride 25. San Leandro — Anthony Chabot Regional Park........ Page 89

Ride 26. San Leandro — Redwood Regional Park .... Page 92

Ride 27. Pleasanton — Pleasanton Ridge Regional Park........ Page 95

Ride 28. Newark — Coyote Hills Regional Park............... Page 98

Ride 29. Livermore — Morgan Territory Regional Preserve .... Page 101

Ride 30. Sunol — Sunol-Ohlone Regional Wilderness .... Page 104

Ride 31. Lafayette — Briones Regional Park .... Page 107

Ride 32. Berkeley — Tilden and Wildcat Canyon Regional Parks Page 110

Ride 33. Danville — Mt. Diablo State Park — Wall Point Road . Page 114

Ride 34. Clayton — Mt. Diablo State Park — Mitchell Canyon . . Page 117

25 San Leandro
Anthony Chabot Regional Park

Difficulty Rating: *Difficult* **Total Distance:** *20 miles*
Skill Level: *Somewhat technical* **Off-Road Distance:** *20 miles*
Elevation Gain: *2,200 feet* **Riding Time:** *3-4 hours*

About the Ride

With a route that covers about 20 miles of trails, this ride completely traverses *Anthony Chabot Regional Park*, located near San Leandro. Beginning at one of the secondary access points to the park, the MacDonald Staging Area along Redwood Road, it initially follows a steep uphill along MacDonald Trail. Expansive views at the crest are brief as the trail drops sharply into the valley below. Passing through Grass Valley along the Brandon Trail, you will often find grazing cattle. A short climb at the end of Grass Valley is followed by a descent to a paved path leading around Lake Chabot. There is usually plenty of activity at this end of the park, since the lake and its diversions attract families with children.

After about 5 miles along the shoreline, you will cross a narrow bridge where you will need to walk your bike. Dirt trails resume at the far side and a steep climb will take you away from the lake and into the remote sections of the park. The route then follows through some camping areas along the crest of the hills and descends back down into Grass Valley for the return along MacDonald Trail.

While there are lots of hills to climb, the trails are generally wide and smooth. Livestock may be present but they are usually quite passive and offer no threat.

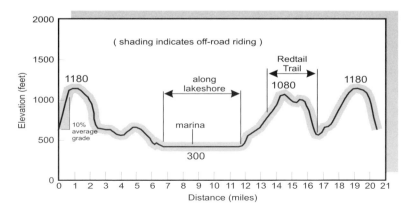

Starting Point

Start the ride at the MacDonald Staging Area in *Anthony Chabot Regional Park* along Redwood Road. To get there, take Highway 13, the Warren Freeway, and get off at the exit for Redwood Road. Follow Redwood Road east up into the hills and continue past the intersection with Skyline Boulevard for about 2 miles. The MacDonald Staging is on the right side.

Mile Markers

0.0 Proceed into the park along MacDonald Trail on the left side in the parking area.

1.1 Turn LEFT to stay on MacDonald Trail.

2.6 Turn LEFT onto the wide trail at the bottom of the hill.

2.7 Turn RIGHT and then LEFT to get on Brandon Trail.

4.1 Turn RIGHT to get on Jackson Grade.

4.6 Continue STRAIGHT ahead onto Goldenrod Trail — Skyline Boulevard gate is on the right side.

5.6 Turn LEFT off the paved section to get on the continuation of Goldenrod Trail.

6.0 Continue STRAIGHT on Bass Cove Trail toward the marina.

7.0 Continue STRAIGHT across the service road and begin West Shore Trail.

8.7 Just past the marina, turn LEFT in the picnic area, cross a wooden bridge, and then turn LEFT onto East Shore Trail.

10.4 Begin dirt trail.

10.6 Turn LEFT and walk your bike across narrow wooden bridge and then turn LEFT onto Honker Bay Trail along leading the lake shore.

11.7 Begin climbing.

12.4 Continue STRAIGHT through the campground along the paved road.

13.0 Just past the park entrance booth, get on Towhee Trail running parallel to the right side of the road.

13.4 Turn LEFT onto Brandon Trail.

13.6 Turn RIGHT onto Redtail Trail, just before the road.

14.0 Cross the road and continue on Redtail Trail.

14.8 Bear RIGHT to stay on Redtail Trail and cross the road.

15.1 Turn RIGHT on the road and then turn LEFT to get on the continuation of Redtail Trail.

16.7 Turn RIGHT onto Grass Valley Trail.

17.6 Continue past the gate toward Bort Meadow and then turn RIGHT onto small trail heading up the hill toward MacDonald Trail.

17.7 Turn LEFT onto MacDonald Trail.

20.3 End of the ride at the parking area.

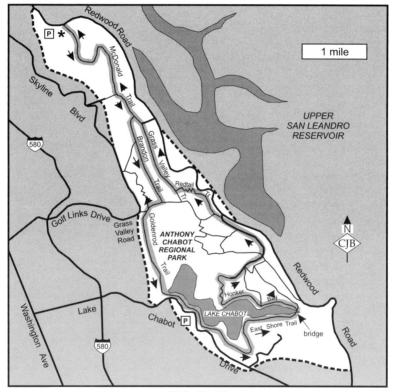

Ride No.25

26 San Leandro
Redwood Regional Park

Difficulty Rating: *Moderate*	**Total Distance:** *10 miles*
Skill Level: *Somewhat technical*	**Off-Road Distance:** *10 miles*
Elevation Gain: *1,200 feet*	**Riding Time:** *2 hours*

About the Ride

Redwood Regional Park is today home to giant redwood trees descended from original growth trees logged long ago. The park terrain consists of a valley surrounded by mountains. While it is rich with trails for hiking, biking, and equestrian use, bikes are restricted to fire roads and must yield at all times to both hikers and equestrians.

The route of this ride follows around the park periphery along the mountain ridges, affording spectacular views from the highest points. Beginning at a trailhead near the park headquarters, it immediately climbs on a steep grade along the West Ridge Trail. Once on the ridge top, the route follows rolling terrain as it loops around the park. After you pass the Roberts Recreation Area and the archery range, the high point of the ride offers the first views down to the central part of the park in the valley below. Once you pass Skyline Gate, the East Ridge Trail leads around the rest of the ridge top and allows you to cruise along a gentle downward grade to get to Canyon Trail and the steep descent back to the valley floor.

The route generally follows wide fire roads with some loose stones. Some very steep sections in the very beginning require most cyclists to walk their bikes for a short distance.

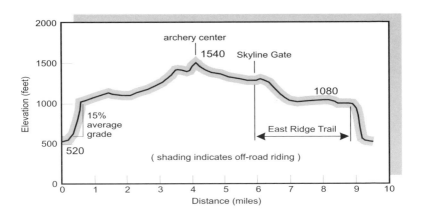

Starting Point

Stare the ride at the main entrance to *Redwood Regional Park* on Redwood Road. To get there, take Highway 13, the Warren Freeway, and get off at the ext for Redwood Road. Follow Redwood Road to the east for about 2 miles to get to the entrance to the park on the left side. Park where you can and begin the ride at the first trailhead on the left side of the road — Bridle Trail — near the Fishway Interpretive Site.

Mile Markers

0.0 Proceed into the park at the trailhead and turn RIGHT onto Bridle Trail.

0.1 Turn LEFT onto West Ridge Trail.

0.4 Golden Spike Trail intersection on the left side.

0.6 Toyon Trail intersection on the left side.

0.9 Orchard Trail intersection on the right side followed by Tate Trail on the left.

1.2 Turn LEFT onto Baccharis Trail.

1.7 Turn LEFT onto Dunn Trail.

2.8 Bear RIGHT to get on Graham Trail.

3.4 Trail to Roberts Park on the left side.

3.9 Turn LEFT to get back on West Ridge Trail.

4.1 Archery center on the right side.

4.2 Continue past the gate to stay on West Ridge Trail.

4.6 Moon Gate on the left side.

4.8 Tres Sendas Trail intersection on the right side.

5.3 French Trail Trail intersection on the right side.

5.9 Continue STRAIGHT ahead at Skyline Gate and begin East Ridge Trail.

7.2 Prince Road intersection on the right side.

8.9 Turn RIGHT onto Canyon Trail and begin descent.

9.3 Turn LEFT onto the paved road to head toward the park entrance.

9.6 End of the ride at the start point.

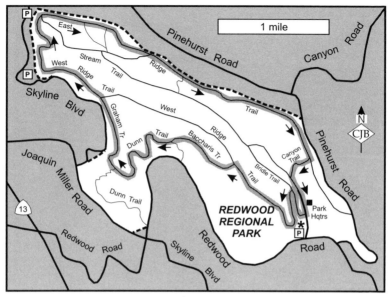

Ride No.26

The view into Redwood Regional Park

27   **Pleasanton**
Pleasanton Ridge Regional Park

Difficulty Rating: *Difficult*   **Total Distance:** *9 miles*
Skill Level: *Somewhat technical*   **Off-Road Distance:** *9 miles*
Elevation Gain: *1,600 feet*   **Riding Time:** *2 hours*

About the Ride

Just to the west of the charming town of Pleasanton lies *Pleasanton Ridge Regional Park*. The peaceful atmosphere of the park stands in sharp contrast to the hectic pace of the car traffic just a few miles away on busy Highway 680. Following along wide fire roads, this ride has plenty of steep terrain. Even along the ridge you can expect to shift gears frequently as you go up and down some rather steep grades.

Leaving the parking area on Oak Tree Trail, the route climbs immediately toward the connection with Ridgeline Trail. Grassy slopes and oak-covered hillsides are the dominant features of the park as Ridgeline Trail continues climbing. Along the ridge, panoramic views to the east into the Livermore Valley reward you for your effort. A conveniently placed picnic table beckons you to rest and to savor the moment.

The open landscape along Ridgeline Trail changes abruptly as you pass through a heavily wooded section just before returning to Ridgeline Trail. The trail returns initially along Ridgeline Trail and then switches to Thermalito Trail with views to the west into Kilkare Canyon, far below. After passing some old ranch buildings, you descend back to the parking area once again along Oak Tree Trail.

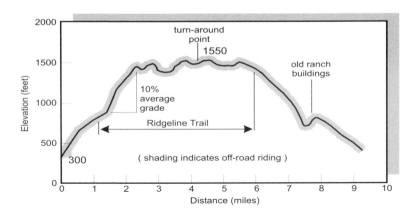

Starting Point

Start the ride at the Oak Tree Staging Area for *Pleasanton Ridge Regional Park*. To get there, take Highway 680 toward Pleasanton and get off at the exit for Bernal Avenue. Go west on Bernal Avenue for a short distance and then turn left onto Foothill Road. The parking area is located on Foothill Road about 3 miles away.

Mile Markers

0.0   Proceed out of the parking area along Oak Tree Trail.

0.6   Intersection with trail to Sycamore Groves on the right side.

1.2   Turn RIGHT and continue past the gate on Oak Tree Trail, then turn RIGHT onto Ridgeline Trail and begin a steep climb.

1.4   Bear RIGHT to stay on Ridgeline Trail.

1.8   Olive Trail intersection on the left side.

2.3   Trail toward Thermalito Trail on the left side.

2.5   Thermalito Trail intersection on the left side.

2.8   Continue past the gate and bear RIGHT to stay on Ridgeline Trail.

2.9   Turn LEFT to stay on Ridgeline Trail.

3.1   Enter Augustine Bernal Park area.

3.7   Continue past the gate and turn RIGHT onto unmarked trail. This will ultimately connect again to Ridgeline Trail.

4.2   Turn LEFT onto Ridgeline Trail to head back.

4.6   Continue past the gate and stay on Ridgeline Trail.

5.5   Continue past another gate.

5.9   Turn RIGHT onto Thermalito Trail.

7.7   Turn LEFT onto Oak Tree Trail.

8.0   Continue STRAIGHT across Ridgeline Trail, pass a gate, and turn LEFT to stay on Oak Tree Trail.

9.4   End of the ride at the parking area.

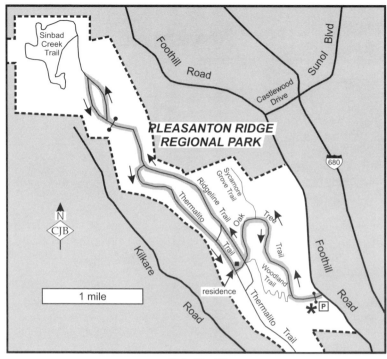

Ride No.27

Ridgeline Trail in Pleasanton Ridge Regional Park

28 Newark
Coyote Hills Regional Park

Difficulty Rating: *Easy*	**Total Distance:** *15 miles*
Skill Level: *Non-technical*	**Off-Road Distance:** *15 miles*
Elevation Gain: *100 feet*	**Riding Time:** *2 hours*

About the Ride

Formerly home to Ohlone Indians for over 2,000 years, *Coyote Hills Regional Park* is today a unique place to experience the wetlands of San Francisco Bay. Crossed with a network of biking and hiking trails, the grassy hillsides of the park stand out against the flat, low-lying land all around. The marshes and mudflats along the coastline are home to insects and marine animals which serve as the food supply for the wide variety of birds frequently seen in the park.

This route takes you into the park and south along the shore of the bay toward the *San Francisco Bay National Wildlife Refuge*, where you can get off your bike and explore the wetlands. The visitor center there has fascinating information about the wetlands. Back in Coyote Hills, the route leads north along Bayview Trail and then out into the bay along the Alameda Creek Regional Trail. Riding along the Shoreline Trail past the salt ponds, you can experience the magnificence of the bay while you view the Dumbarton Bridge in the distance. The return to the park is again along the Bayview Trail as it follows along the shoreline. Through the marshes and past the Indian Mound Archaeological Site, you return to the parking area.

The ride is quite easy and flat as it follows along mostly paved trails, except for some stretches of gravel.

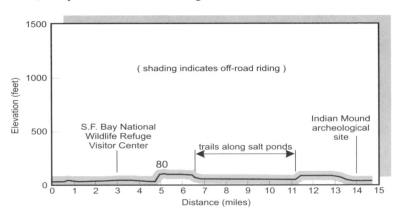

Starting Point

Start the ride at the parking lot at the entrance to *Coyote Hills Regional Park*. To get there, take Highway 880 to Newark and get off at the exit for Highway 84 and the Dumbarton Bridge. Head west on Highway 84 toward the bridge and get off at Ardenwood Boulevard. Proceed north along Ardenwood Boulevard, turn left onto Paseo Padre Parkway and then right onto Paterson Ranch Road. Follow this road to the park entrance.

Mile Markers

0.0   Proceed WEST out of the parking area into Coyote Hills Regional Park along the paved trail that runs parallel to the roadway.

0.4   Turn LEFT onto Bayview Trail and cross the road.

0.9   Bear LEFT to stay on the paved trail.

1.1   Bear RIGHT toward Shoreline Trail and Apay Way.

1.2   Turn LEFT onto San Francisco Bay Trail — Apay Way.

2.6   Cross over Highway 84 on the overpass.

3.6   San Francisco Bay National Wildlife Center visitor center. Stop to explore and then return the way you came.

4.8   Turn LEFT onto Bayview Trail.

6.5   Turn LEFT toward Alameda Creek and then turn LEFT onto Alameda Creek Regional Trail to head west toward the bay.

8.7   Begin Shoreline Trail in San Francisco Bay National Wildlife Refuge. Dumbarton Bridge is visible ahead.

9.6   Continue STRAIGHT toward Coyote Hills. Shoreline Trail turns to the right at this point.

11.5   Turn LEFT onto Bayview Trail back in Coyote Hills Regional Park.

13.2   Continue STRAIGHT along Bayview Trail at the point where Alameda Creek Trail access is to the left.

13.6   Turn LEFT onto Lizard Rock Trail toward Chochenyo Trail.

13.8   Turn LEFT onto unmarked trail.

14.0   Turn RIGHT onto unmarked trail through the marsh and then LEFT onto Chochenyo Trail toward Indian Mound.

14.3   Turn RIGHT to go around the Indian Mound Archaeological Site.

14.4   Bear RIGHT at the far end of the site.

14.8   End of the ride at the parking area.

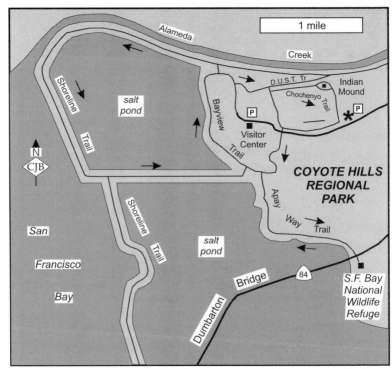

Ride No.28

The salt ponds of Coyote Hills Park

29   Livermore
Morgan Territory Regional Preserve

Difficulty Rating: *Easy*	**Total Distance:** *7 miles*
Skill Level: *Non-technical*	**Off-Road Distance:** *7 miles*
Elevation Gain: *600 feet*	**Riding Time:** *1-2 hours*

About the Ride

Just north of Livermore lies a quiet country road leading toward Clayton along the eastern slope of Mt. Diablo. Morgan Territory Road is about as remote as you can get in the Bay Area, considering how near to the population centers it is. *Morgan Territory Regional Preserve*, located on the top of the hill on Morgan Territory Road, is tiny in comparison to nearby *Mt. Diablo State Park*. Its small size and relative obscurity offer the mountain bike enthusiast a chance to experience classic East Bay trails without crowds.

This ride will lead you on a fairly complete tour of the preserve. Starting at the main park entrance at 1,900 feet elevation, the cyclist immediately is rewarded with panoramic views without the usual effort required by an extended climb. Proceeding initially along the wide Volvon and Blue Oak Trails, the route suddenly leads steeply downhill along Valley View Trail. True to its name, Valley View Trail offers stunning vistas to the east into the San Joaquin Valley and toward Discovery Bay and the Delta. The climb back up has several short and steep sections, but is generally not very difficult. The Volvon Loop Trail then leads back to Volvon Trail for the return to the starting point.

Watch for equestrians and always slow down as you approach, since horses can sometimes spook easily. The summers can be quite hot in the East Bay, so be prepared with adequate water.

Starting Point

Start the ride at the main entrance for *Morgan Territory Regional Preserve*. To get there, take Highway 580 to Livermore and get off at the exit for North Livermore Avenue. Follow North Livermore Avenue about 4 miles north and then turn right onto Morgan Territory Road. The preserve is on top of the hill about 6 miles distant.

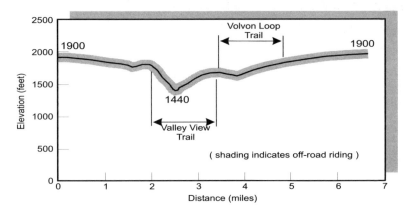

Mile Markers

0.0 Proceed into the preserve along Volvon Trail.

0.3 Continue along Volvon Trail as it merges with a fire road coming in from the right side.

0.6 Turn LEFT to stay on Volvon Trail and then bear RIGHT onto Blue Oak Trail.

1.2 Bear LEFT to stay on Blue Oak Trail — Manzanita Trail is to the right.

1.4 Bear RIGHT to stay on Blue Oak Trail — Hummingbird Trail branches to the left.

2.0 Turn RIGHT onto Volvon Trail.

2.1 Continue past the gate and then turn RIGHT onto Valley View Trail.

2.8 Views into the central valley.

3.2 Continue STRAIGHT toward Volvon Loop Trail.

3.3 Turn RIGHT onto Volvon Loop Trail.

4.0 Turn LEFT to stay on Volvon Loop Trail — Eagle Trail branches to the right.

4.6 Pass through the livestock gate and continue STRAIGHT — Valley View Trail is to the left.

5.3 Turn RIGHT to stay on Volvon Trail — Hummingbird Trail is on the left.

6.0 Turn RIGHT to stay on Volvon Trail — Blue Oak Trail is on the left.

6.7 End of the ride at the parking area.

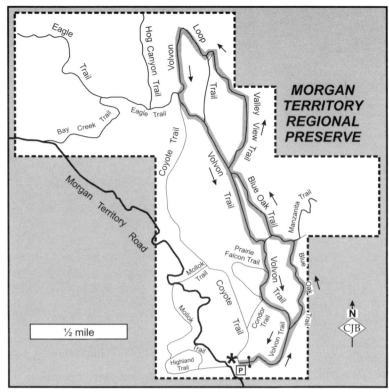

Ride No.29

Valley View Trail in Morgan Territory

30 Sunol
Sunol-Ohlone Regional Wilderness

Difficulty Rating: *Difficult*	**Total Distance:** *10 miles*
Skill Level: *Somewhat technical*	**Off-Road Distance:** *9 miles*
Elevation Gain: *2,000 feet*	**Riding Time:** *3 hours*

About the Ride

Several hundred years ago, Ohlone Indians lived and prospered in a valley in the East Bay, just east of what is now Sunol. More recently, the valley was used for cattle ranching. Today, the *Sunol-Ohlone Regional Wilderness*, administered by the East Bay Regional Parks District, is open to the general public for recreational use. While the land is still used for cattle grazing, its primary purpose has changed to offer a variety of outdoor activities, like camping, backpacking, hiking, horseback riding and mountain biking. Although it is relatively unknown outside of the East Bay, the *Sunol-Ohlone Regional Wilderness* contains many miles of trails, mostly over rugged terrain. Views of the nearby Calaveras Reservoir are rewards for those stalwart individuals willing to venture to the higher elevations within the park.

This ride will take you from the park headquarters along a flat fire road toward "Little Yosemite", a picturesque camping area at the east end of the park. Before reaching the campgrounds, the route turns and heads uphill along a steep trail to the Cerro Este Overlook, the highest spot on the ride. Eagle View Trail and Cave Rocks Trail lead you along the ridge and down to High Valley where an old barn remains. Another climb along Vista Grande Road will take you to paved Welch Creek Road and a fast descent to get to the trailhead for Flag Hill Road. Flag Hill Road returns you to High Valley and then down the hill back to park headquarters.

While the terrain is quite steep in places, the trails are wide. Since they may not be clearly marked, it is importantly to follow the route directions carefully. Grazing cattle are common within the park, but they are normally quite passive.

Starting Point

Start the ride at the main parking area in *Sunol-Ohlone Regional Wilderness*. To get there, take Highway 680 toward Sunol and get off at the exit for Calaveras Road. Be sure to take the exit for Calaveras Road in Sunol, as there is an exit, Calaveras Boulevard, in Milpitas also. Follow Calaveras Road east for about 4 miles and then turn left into the park along Geary Road. The park is 2 miles in on Geary Road.

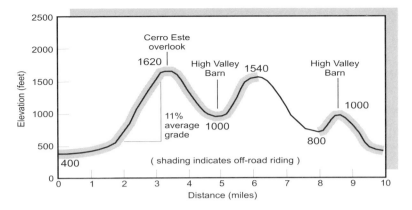

Mile Markers

0.0 Proceed into the park along the paved road, heading toward Little Yosemite.

0.5 Continue past the gate, cross over a bridge and follow Camp Ohlone Road.

1.6 Turn LEFT onto Cerro Este Road and begin steep climb.

2.6 McCorkle Trail intersection on the left side.

3.0 McCorkle Trail intersection on the right side.

3.4 Turn LEFT onto Cave Rocks Road. Cerro Este Overlook is on the left side with expansive views to Calaveras Reservoir to the south.

4.0 Continue STRAIGHT ahead to get on Cave Rocks Road as Eagle View Trail branches off to the right.

4.8 Just after High Valley Camp, bear RIGHT to stay on Cave Rocks Road.

5.1 Turn RIGHT onto Vista Grande Road toward upper Welch Creek Road.

6.2 Turn LEFT onto Eagle View Trail as Vista Grande Road continues straight ahead.

6.6 Turn LEFT onto paved Welch Creek Road and begin descent.

7.4 Cross cattle guard.

7.9 Turn LEFT onto unmarked High Valley Road.

8.4 Continue STRAIGHT on High Valley Road at the intersection with Vista Grande Road on the left.

8.6 Bear RIGHT at High Valley Camp and begin steep descent along Hayfield Road.

9.9 Turn RIGHT at the end of Hayfield Road and then turn LEFT immediately to cross the stream.

10.0 End of the ride at the parking area.

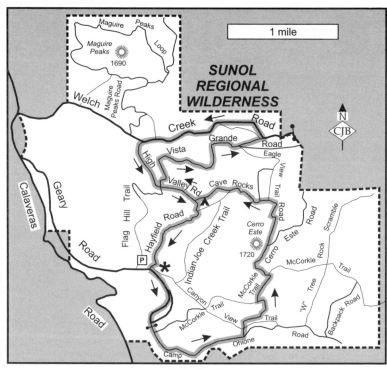

Ride No.30

The hills of Sunol-Ohlone Regional Wilderness

31 Lafayette
Briones Regional Park

Difficulty Rating: *Difficult*	Total Distance: *10 miles*
Skill Level: *Somewhat technical*	**Off-Road Distance:** *10 miles*
Elevation Gain: *1,700 feet*	**Riding Time:** *2-3 hours*

About the Ride

In the early 1800's, the land in what today is *Briones Regional Park* was settled by Felipe Briones. After passing through the hands of other owners, the property was eventually acquired as a part of the larger East Bay watershed and later still, was transferred to the East Bay Regional Park District for use as recreational open space.

This ride consists of a tour of *Briones Regional Park*, following the ridges high above and around the park as much as possible. Stunning views of the distant countryside in all directions add to the grandeur this strenuous ride. Grass- and oak-covered slopes, heavily forested canyons, and the occasional meadow will stimulate the visual senses.

After passing through a small meadow at the beginning of the ride, the route then climbs steeply along Crescent Ridge Trail. Views along Briones Crest Trail and from Briones Peak are followed by a gradual descent to the far entrance of the park. After a short section along a paved section, the route then follows Pine Tree Trail to Toyon Canyon Trail and another steep climb, this time up to Mott Peak. The steep descent along Black Oak Trail leads to another meadow and the return on Old Briones Road to the parking area.

The route follows wide fire roads across hills that are quite steep in places. Trails are well-marked and trail maps are usually available at the park entrances.

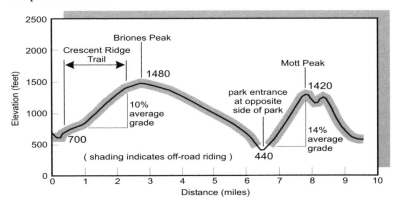

Starting Point

Start the ride in the parking area at the Bear Creek Road entrance to *Briones Regional Park*. To get there, take Highway 24 to Lafayette and get off at the exit for Pleasant Hill Road. Go south on Pleasant Hill Road and then turn right onto Mt. Diablo Boulevard. Follow Mt. Diablo Boulevard for about 1½ miles and then turn right onto Happy Valley Road. After about 4 miles, Happy Valley Road ends at Bear Creek Road. Turn right and look for the park entrance on the right side.

Mile Markers

0.0   Proceed out of the parking area along Old Briones Road.

0.1   Just past the gate, turn RIGHT onto Homestead Valley Trail.

0.4   Continue past a gate and through a meadow and then turn LEFT onto Crescent Ridge Trail.

0.9   Archery range is on the right side — steep climb begins.

1.7   Bear RIGHT to stay on Crescent Ridge Trail.

2.2   Continue past the gate and then turn LEFT onto Briones Crest Trail.

2.7   Bear LEFT at the intersection with Table Top Trail on the right to stay on Briones Crest Trail.

4.2   Turn RIGHT onto Old Briones Road.

4.7   Bear LEFT at the intersection with Spengler Trail on the right to stay on Old Briones Road.

5.4   Continue past the gate onto the paved road.

5.8   Turn LEFT onto Pine Tree Trail at the gate on the left side of the road.

6.2   Turn LEFT onto Toyon Canyon Trail.

7.0   Bear LEFT onto Lagoon Trail.

7.6   Turn RIGHT onto Mott Peak Trail.

7.8   Bear LEFT to stay on Mott Peak Trail.

8.1   Turn LEFT onto Black Oak Trail.

8.9   Turn RIGHT onto Old Briones Road.

9.4   Continue past the gate and back to the start point.

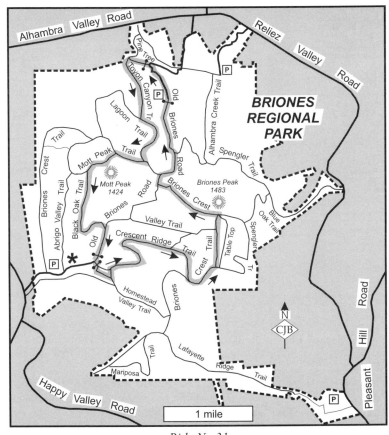

Ride No.31

Briones Regional Park

32 **Berkeley**

Tilden and Wildcat Canyon Regional Parks

Difficulty Rating: *Moderate*	**Total Distance:** *17 miles*
Skill Level: *Somewhat technical*	**Off-Road Distance:** *16 miles*
Elevation Gain: *1,700 feet*	**Riding Time:** *2-3 hours*

About the Ride

Just to the east of Berkeley and up into the Berkeley Hills, are the adjacent parks, *Tilden Regional Park* and *Wildcat Canyon Regional Park*. Tilden Park includes a golf course, botanical garden, steam trains, pony rides, merry-go-round, nature area, and Lake Anza. Weekends find the parks heavily used as residents from the surrounding areas come to relax and enjoy the many diversions available. Despite the large number of visitors, it is quite easy to get away from the crowds once you are on the many trails in these two marvelous parks.

The first part of this ride consists of a short 4-mile loop through the southern section of Tilden Park. This section includes a fairly steep 500-foot climb and less ambitious riders might want to avoid it and begin the ride at the start of the longer loop at 3.9 miles. The long loop leads through the northern part of Tilden Park and then extends into Wildcat Canyon Park. The first 4 miles follow a paved pathway along Chester Nimitz Way, named for the famous World War II admiral. Along this relatively flat section at the top of the ridgeline, there are stunning views of the surrounding areas in both directions. At the end of the paved trail, the route follows along fire roads as it continues on the crest of the hills and then descends down a steep trail into Wildcat Canyon. After riding through the canyon in the lower elevations of the park, the route leads past serene Jewel Lake and then follows a forested trail back uphill to Inspiration Point and the start point of the ride.

The trails in both parks are wide fire roads that are steep in some sections and often can be rough and bumpy.

Starting Point

Start the ride at Inspiration Point on Wildcat Canyon Road. To get there from the east, take Highway 24 to the exit for Orinda and follow Camino Pablo north. Turn left onto Wildcat Canyon Road and follow it about 2½ miles to Inspiration Point, at the top of the ridge on the right side.

From the west, take Ashby Avenue, in Berkeley, east to Claremont Avenue and up into the Berkeley Hills. Turn left onto Grizzly Peak Boulevard and then right onto South Park Drive. Turn right again onto

Wildcat Canyon Road and look for Inspiration Point at the top of the hill, about 1½ miles distant.

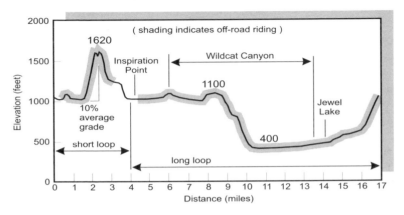

Mile Markers

0.0 Start the ***short loop*** by heading out of the parking area at Inspiration Point and turn RIGHT onto Wildcat Canyon Road.

0.4 Turn LEFT into the Quarry Picnic Area and follow the trails sign, just past the picnic table.

0.7 Bear RIGHT to stay on Quarry Trail.

1.5 Continue STRAIGHT to get on Big Springs Trail and proceed past the parking lot to continue the trail at the far end.

2.0 Turn LEFT onto Seaview Trail which runs along the ridge.

3.3 Intersection with Big Springs Trail on the left side.

3.7 Turn RIGHT onto Wildcat Canyon Road at the end of the trail.

3.9 Turn LEFT to end the ***short loop*** back at Inspiration Point. Begin the ***long loop*** by continuing into Tilden Park through the gate and onto paved Nimitz Way.

5.8 Cross cattle guard to enter Wildcat Canyon Park.

6.1 Intersection with Conlon Trail on the left side.

8.0 Veer LEFT onto gravel trail and continue past the gate.

8.2 Turn LEFT onto Mezue Trail and then RIGHT onto San Pablo Ridge Trail.

9.4 Bear LEFT onto Belgum Trail.

9.5 Intersection with Clark Boas Trail on the right side.

10.3 Continue past the gate and then turn LEFT onto the unimproved road toward Tilden Nature Area.

11.1 Turn RIGHT off the road and continue on paved section to the gravel trail just ahead.

13.5 Enter Tilden Nature Area.

14.3   Bear LEFT just past Jewel Lake onto Loop Trail.

14.8   Bear RIGHT to stay on Loop Trail.

15.1   Turn LEFT to stay on Loop Trail and continue past the gate onto paved road.

15.3   Turn LEFT at the Lone Oak Picnic Ground to get on fire trail and then bear RIGHT onto Wildcat Gorge Trail.

16.1   Turn LEFT onto Curran Trail.

16.6   Bear RIGHT at the intersection with Meadows Canyon Trail on the left side.

16.4   End of the ride back at Inspiration Point.

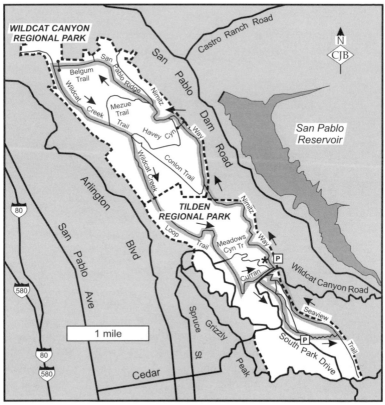

Ride No. 32

33 Danville
Mt. Diablo State Park — Wall Point Road

Difficulty Rating: *Difficult*	**Total Distance:** *9 miles*
Skill Level: *Somewhat technical*	**Off-Road Distance:** *8 miles*
Elevation Gain: *1,800 feet*	**Riding Time:** *2-3 hours*

About the Ride

Dominating the landscape in the East Bay, Mt. Diablo towers to a height of 3,849 feet and can be seen from nearly anywhere in the Bay Area. Easily the largest park in the Bay Area, *Mt. Diablo State Park* offers visitors many miles of trails for hiking, cycling, and horseback riding. This ride is located in the western part of the park and is easily accessible near Alamo and Danville. It is an ideal introduction to the park by virtue of the wide variety of terrain and geology along the way and the stunning views of the distant summit above and population centers below.

Starting at the historic Macedo Ranch staging area, the route first leads uphill through pasture land where it is common to encounter grazing cattle. After this short climb, a short descent follows and then a more extended climb along Wall Point Road. Wall Point Road is a wide fire road that leads along the ridge line to Rock City, a camping and day-use area with some fascinating geology. Be sure to savor the views in both directions along the climb up Wall Point Road. At Rock City the climb continues along single-track running parallel to the road. A short stretch along the road leads to Barbeque Terrace, a popular camping area, and then a long downhill on BBQ Terrace Road. At the bottom, the trail then follows through a shady canyon and leads to one final hill to overcome to get back to Macedo Ranch.

The route follows wide fire roads, often quite steep, with loose gravel in some places. A short single-track section will provide some challenge for intermediate riders. Trails are not always clearly marked, so it is important to follow the directions closely.

Starting Point

Stare the ride at the Macedo Ranch staging area in *Mt. Diablo State Park* at the end of Green Valley Road near Danville. To get there take Highway 680 to Danville and get off at the exit for Stone Valley Road. Go east about 3 miles along Stone Valley Road and then turn left onto Green Valley Road. At the end of Green Valley Road is the Macedo Ranch staging area with parking and restrooms.

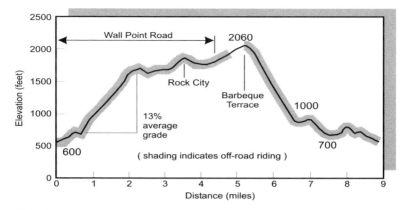

(shading indicates off-road riding)

Mile Markers

0.0 Proceed past the gate into the park along Wall Point Road and begin climbing immediately.

0.3 Bear RIGHT to stay on Wall Point Road.

0.6 Top of the first hill.

0.8 Continue past the gate and turn RIGHT to stay on Wall Point Road.

1.2 Bear LEFT to stay on Wall Point Road. To the right is Emmons Canyon Road.

1.8 Rock formations come into view on right side.

3.3 Trail intersection on the left side and Rock City formations come into view on the right side

3.8 Trail to Rock City on the right side. Bikes are not permitted.

4.0 Just before the main road, turn LEFT onto Summit Trail and climb some more.

4.3 As trail comes back to the road, turn LEFT to stay on Summit Trail.

4.6 Continue STRAIGHT at trail intersections on each side.

5.0 Turn LEFT onto main road as the trail ends.

5.2 Turn LEFT onto paved road and then bear LEFT immediately at a split to continue toward Barbeque Terrace camping area.

5.5 Just before the camping area, turn LEFT and continue past the gate onto Barbeque Terrace Road.

7.8 Turn LEFT onto unmarked trail which goes steeply uphill to connect to Wall Point Road. The road to the right crosses a stream at this point and is NOT the way to go.

8.3 As Continue STRAIGHT at the intersection with Wall Point Road. Go past the gate back toward Macedo Ranch.

8.8 Bear LEFT to stay on Wall Point Road.

9.0 End of the ride at Macedo Ranch staging area.

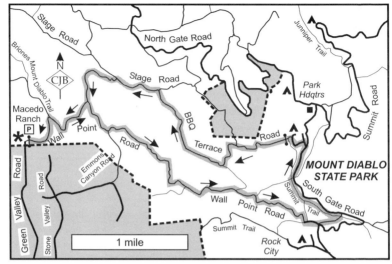

Ride No.33

The rolling hills of Mt. Diablo

34 Clayton

Mt. Diablo State Park — Mitchell Canyon

Difficulty Rating: *Difficult*	**Total Distance:** *9 miles*
Skill Level: *Very technical*	**Off-Road Distance:** *9 miles*
Elevation *1,900 feet*	**Riding Time:** *2 hours*

About the Ride

Rising to an elevation of 3,849 feet, Mt. Diablo is a dominating presence in the East Bay as it towers over the surrounding hills and flatlands. Trails and fire roads within *Mt. Diablo State Park* provide hikers, equestrians and mountain bikers with innumerable routes from which to choose.

The eastern side of the park, near the town of Clayton, is the location of this ride. Somewhat isolated from the larger population centers on the other side of the mountain, the trails around Clayton normally carry much less traffic. The Mitchell Canyon entrance to the park is the starting point of the ride. The route begins with a gentle uphill grade leading through Mitchell Canyon. The steep hillsides on each side of the trail offer a feeling of protection and tranquility as you gradually warm up your legs through this section. At the end of the canyon, about 2 miles into the ride, the trail leads uphill more steeply. Expect to use your lowest gears as the trail climbs for about 1½ miles along a 14% grade. At Deer Flat there is a short downhill section before an even steeper climb. The descent back down the mountain is also quite steep and may even require you to lower your saddle for added safety. The views toward Clayton are quite spectacular on this side of the hill. The ride ends with a flat stretch through rolling grassland back to the start point.

While the fire roads are generally quite wide and usually have smooth surfaces, the steepness of both the uphill and downhill grades makes the ride quite challenging. It can be very hot in the summer months, so maintaining hydration is a necessity.

Starting Point

Start the ride at the Mitchell Canyon entrance to *Mt. Diablo State Park*. Get there by taking either Highway 680 or Highway 24 to Walnut Creek. Get of Highway 680 at Ygnacio Valley Road and follow it east through Walnut Creek to Clayton. Turn right on Clayton Road for about 1½ miles and then turn right onto Mitchell Canyon Road. At the end of the road is the park entrance with parking and restrooms.

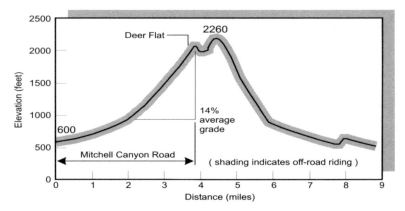

Mile Markers

0.0 Proceed into the park along Mitchell Canyon Trail.

1.0 Fire Road intersection on the right side.

2.0 Steep climb begins.

3.6 Picnic tables on the right side — Deer Flat.

3.8 Bear LEFT onto Prospector's Gap Fire Road toward North Peak.

4.5 Eagle Peak Trail intersection on the left side.

4.9 Turn LEFT onto Meridian Ridge Trail toward Donner Canyon Trail and begin a very steep descent.

5.7 Meridian Point Trail intersection on the left side.

6.3 Turn LEFT onto Donner Canyon Trail toward Regency Gate.

7.6 Just after an unmarked fire road on the right side, the Regency Gate is straight ahead. Turn LEFT onto another unmarked fire road.

7.8 Continue STRAIGHT ahead where there are trail intersections on both side.

8.1 Continue STRAIGHT at the 4-way trail intersection and follow parallel to the wood fence on the right side of the trail.

8.7 Continue STRAIGHT at another 4-way trail intersection to the parking area ahead.

8.8 End of the ride at the parking area.

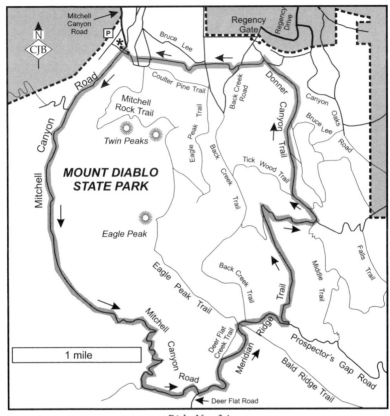

Ride No. 34

Mt. Diablo State Park

The North Bay

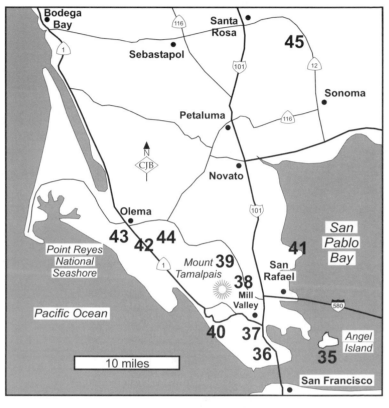

Ride 35. San Francisco — Angel Island State Park . . . . Page 121

Ride 36. San Francisco — Marin Headlands . . . . Page 124

Ride 37. Mill Valley — Tennessee Valley and Muir Beach . . . . . Page 127

Ride 38. Mill Valley — Mt. Tamalpais — East Peak Loop . . . . . . Page 130

Ride 39. Ross — Mt. Tamalpais Watershed — Lakes Loop . . . . . Page 133

Ride 40. Muir Beach — Mt. Tamalpais and Muir Woods . . . . Page 136

Ride 41. San Rafael — China Camp . . . . Page 139

Ride 42. Olema — Bolinas Ridge and Point Reyes . . . . Page 142

Ride 43. Olema — Point Reyes National Seashore Bike & Hike . Page 145

Ride 44. Lagunitas — Samuel P. Taylor State Park
and Bolinas Ridge Loop . . . . Page 148

Ride 45. Santa Rosa — Annadel State Park . . . . Page 151

35 San Francisco
Angel Island State Park

Difficulty Rating: *Easy*	**Total Distance:** *11 miles*
Skill Level: *Non-technical*	**Off-Road Distance:** *11 miles*
Elevation Gain: *700 feet*	**Riding Time:** *2 hours*

About the Ride

One of the most unusual — and certainly one of the most pleasantly situated — state parks in California is *Angel Island State Park*. Located in San Francisco Bay, Angel Island has had a long and varied history. The earliest known use was as a home of native-Americans. Later, the island was used militarily in both the Civil War and World War II. It also served as an immigration center and for Nike missile defense. Today its use as a state park allows us to enjoy its unique beauty and to re-live its history through its museums and points of interest.

This ride starts at the dock area located at Ayala Cove, the place where the ferries arrive from San Francisco and Tiburon. It first circles about ¾ of the way around the island along a paved road. Spectacular views of the beautiful San Francisco Bay and fascinating points of interest along the way make this the kind of ride that needs to be done at a leisurely pace. The route then leads uphill along a wide fire road to a trail that also encircles the island. At the completion of this second loop, the route descends back to the paved road for the return to Ayala Cove.

The island has no public car traffic. The trails are smooth and the climbs are modest, allowing this ride to be done by beginners to the sport of mountain biking. The sights and history on the island should appeal to advanced riders as well, even though the ride itself is an easy one.

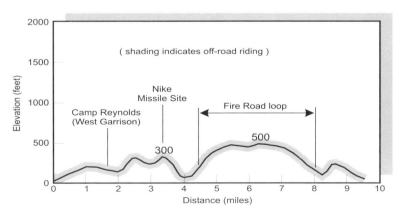

Starting Point

Access to Angel Island is by ferry, either from San Francisco or from Tiburon. From San Francisco, the *Blue and Gold Fleet* has regularly-scheduled trips leaving from Pier 41 (phone number is 415-773-1188). From Tiburon, use the *Tiburon — Angel Island Ferry Company* (phone number is 415-435-2131). Call the ferry company you plan to use for schedules and directions.

Mile Markers

0.0 Proceed from the ferry dock to the right along the waterfront. Look for signs directing you to Perimeter Road.

0.2 Turn LEFT onto the bike path and head uphill.

0.6 Turn RIGHT onto Perimeter Road.

1.4 Turn RIGHT into Camp Reynolds (West Garrison.) Proceed down to the water's edge at Point Stuart.

1.8 Turn around at Point Stuart.

2.2 Turn RIGHT back onto Perimeter Road.

2.6 Trail intersection on right side to Perles Beach.

2.7 Unmarked trail on the left side.

2.9 Old rock quarry on left side.

3.0 Turn LEFT toward Battery Drew.

3.3 Continue STRAIGHT ahead onto Perimeter Road.

3.7 Turn RIGHT at 4-way intersection to stay on Perimeter Road.

4.0 Nike missile site on the left side.

4.5 Continue STRAIGHT through Fort McDowell (East Garrison.).

4.7 Remains of old hospital on the left side.

5.0 Turn LEFT just after fire house on the left side and proceed uphill on gravel road.

5.4 Bear RIGHT at the split to follow the posted bike route.

5.5 Continue along the fire road along the right side of the island water supply.

6.0 Trail intersection on the left side.

6.9 Another trail intersection on the left side.

7.3 Another trail intersection on the left side.

8.3 Turn LEFT on the paved road and then RIGHT to get back on the fire road.

8.7 Continue STRAIGHT at the end of the fire road loop and descend back to Perimeter Road.

9.1 Turn LEFT onto Perimeter Road.

10.3 Turn RIGHT sharply to get back on the bike path leading down into the cove.

10.7 End of the ride.

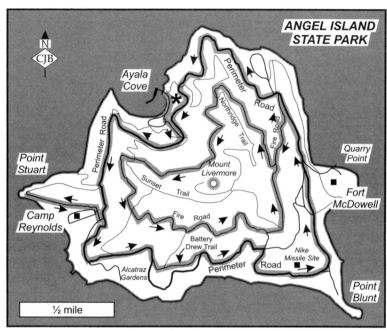

Ride No.35

Ayala Cove on Angel Island

36 San Francisco
Marin Headlands

Difficulty Rating: *Difficult*	**Total Distance:** *24 miles*
Skill Level: *Somewhat technical*	**Off-Road Distance:** *10 miles*
Elevation Gain: *2,800 feet*	**Riding Time:** *3-4 hours*

About the Ride

During World War II the nation's defenses included major anti-aircraft installation along the Pacific Coast to protect against attack from foreign aircraft. Some remnants of those times are present today just north of San Francisco across the Golden Gate Bridge.

The *Golden Gate National Recreation Area* includes what is more commonly known as the Marin Headlands. The hills of the headlands, easily seen on the west side of Highway 101 across the bridge from the city, are home not only to the decaying battlements, but also to many trails and fire roads which meander across them and through the canyons of this public-use land. Long a favorite of San Francisco hikers and equestrians, the Marin Headlands has more recently become a play area for the many mountain bike enthusiasts of the Bay Area.

The route of this ride begins on the San Francisco side of the Golden Gate Bridge, since that side is where most of the users of Marin Headlands come from. It could just as easily begin on the Marin side, since there is plenty of public parking available there as well. After crossing the bridge, the route leads up along the main paved road toward the Battery 129 at Hawk Hill and then down the other side to Fort Cronkhite and Rodeo Beach. After a short stop at the beach, you get back on the trails and climb the hill along Miwok Trail to then descend into Tennessee Valley, the main jumping-off point for the headlands. Another climb along Marincello trail yields panoramic views of Richardson Bay and Sausalito before dropping down again near Fort Cronkhite. One final climb takes you back up to the road leading back to Golden Gate Bridge.

The trails are wide, generally smooth, and not terribly steep. There are four distinct climbs along the route however, and that is what makes the ride somewhat strenuous.

Starting Point

Start the ride on the San Francisco side of the Golden Gate Bridge, on Merchant Road near the toll station. To get there, take Highway 101 as if you were going north across the bridge. Get off at the vista point right at the toll booth, go through the parking lot and then turn right

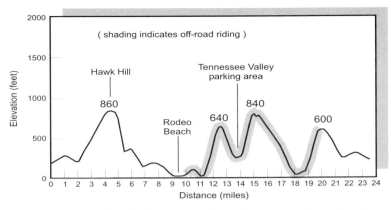

(shading indicates off-road riding)

onto Lincoln Boulevard. Cross under the bridge approach road and turn right on Merchant Road. Park along the road.

If you are coming from the North Bay, begin the ride at the north side of the bridge and pick up the directions at the 2.2 mile point.

Mile Markers

0.0 Proceed through the tunnel under the bridge roadway and head NORTH across the bridge. Follow the signs for bicyclists.

2.2 At the north end of the bridge, turn LEFT onto Conzelman Road, leading up the hill.

3.6 Bear LEFT to stay on Conzelman Road at the intersection with McCullogh Road on the right side.

4.2 Battery 129 and Hawk Hill on the right side.

6.5 Continue STRAIGHT at the intersection to head toward Point Bonita.

6.9 Turn LEFT on the main road toward the lighthouse.

7.0 Point Bonita Lighthouse on the left side — continue STRAIGHT.

7.3 End of the road with views — return along the road.

8.8 Turn LEFT just after the visitor center.

9.3 Bear LEFT toward the Rodeo Beach.

9.8 End of the road at Rodeo Beach — return along the road.

10.5 Just past the last building in Fort Cronkhite on the left side, turn LEFT and proceed on Miwok Trail.

10.8 Continue STRAIGHT at the intersection with Rodeo Valley Trail on the right side.

11.0 Continue STRAIGHT at the intersection with Bobcat Trail on the right side.

12.4 Turn LEFT onto Old Springs Trail.

13.6 Continue through the stables area toward parking lot.

13.8 Turn RIGHT onto Marincello Trail just after the Miwok Trail intersection.

15.3 Bear LEFT to get on Bobcat Trail.

16.0 Bear RIGHT to stay on Bobcat Trail.

18.1 Turn LEFT onto Rodeo Valley Trail.

18.3 Bear RIGHT at the trail split.

18.5 Cross a small bridge and then turn LEFT onto the paved road.

18.7 Cross the main road and then get on the trail on the far side. Continue through the clearing and then turn LEFT onto Coastal Trail

20.3 Continue past the gate and turn LEFT onto Conzelman Road to return to the Golden Gate Bridge.

21.4 Turn RIGHT onto the road leading back to the bridge and continue across to San Francisco.

23.7 End of the ride at the staring point.

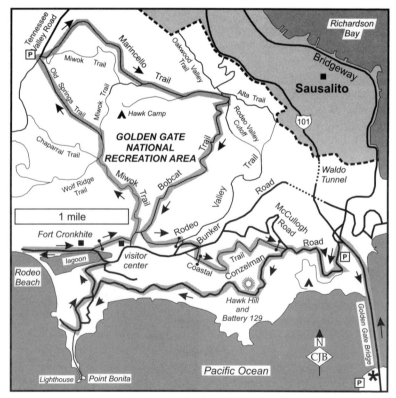

Ride No.36

37 Mill Valley
Tennessee Valley and Muir Beach

Difficulty Rating: *Difficult*	**Total Distance:** *11 miles*
Skill Level: *Somewhat technical*	**Off-Road Distance:** *9 miles*
Elevation Gain: *1,700 feet*	**Riding Time:** *2 hours*

About the Ride

Just across the Golden Gate Bridge from San Francisco lies the Marin Headlands, a part of the *Golden Gate National Recreation Area.* The many trails and fire roads in the headlands have long been popular with cyclists, hikers and equestrians.

Staring at the main staging area in Tennessee Valley, this route loops around the northern part of the Marin Headlands. Weekends often find the Tennessee Valley parking lot full, so it may be necessary to park nearby and ride in. The route initially follows the Tennessee Valley Trail from the parking area toward the beach. Coastal Trail then climbs sharply away from the main trail before the beach. Coastal Fire Road leads steeply downhill, offering some expansive views of the ocean before finally reaching Muir Beach where there are restrooms and picnic areas. A two-mile stretch along busy Highway 1 is necessary to reach the trailhead for Miwok Trail and a spectacular cruise along the ridge back to Tennessee Valley.

While there are some steep climbs along the route, they are not extremely long ones. The highest point in the ride is only about 900 feet above sea level. The most difficult riding is along some of the downhill sections, which can be steep and bumpy.

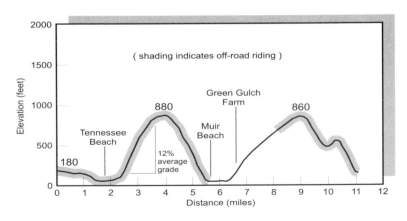

Starting Point

Start the ride at the Tennessee Valley parking area in Marin Head-lands. Get there by taking Highway 101 to southern Marin County. Get off at the exit for Highway 1 and continue toward Stinson Beach. Follow Highway 1 for about a mile and then turn left onto Tennessee Valley Road. The parking area is located about 2 miles in.

Mile Markers

0.0   Proceed WEST along Tennessee Valley Trail, heading toward the beach.

1.2   Continue STRAIGHT at the intersection with Coastal Trail on the right side.

1.8   Tennessee Beach — return back along Tennessee Valley Trail.

2.4   Turn LEFT onto Coastal Trail and begin climbing.

3.1   Turn RIGHT onto Coastal Fire Road toward Coyote Ridge Trail.

3.9   Turn LEFT to stay on Coastal Fire Road (Fox Trail is to the right) and then continue STRAIGHT again to stay on Coastal Fire Road at the intersection with Coyote Ridge Trail on the right side.

5.3   Continue STRAIGHT at the intersection with Green Gulch Trail on the right side and then follow the trail as it turns to the right to head toward the road

5.7   Turn RIGHT onto the unmarked road toward Highway 1 and then turn RIGHT onto Highway 1. This part of Highway 1 is often very busy with traffic and has no shoulder, so be very careful and stay to the right.

7.8   At the top of the hill, turn RIGHT onto Miwok Trail.

9.4   Turn LEFT to stay on Miwok Trail at the intersection with Coyote Ridge Trail on the right side.

10.0   Turn RIGHT to stay on Miwok Trail.

10.2   Just after the trail intersection on the right side, turn RIGHT to stay on Miwok Trail toward Tennessee Valley.

10.6   Begin steep and narrow descent.

11.2   End of the ride at the parking area.

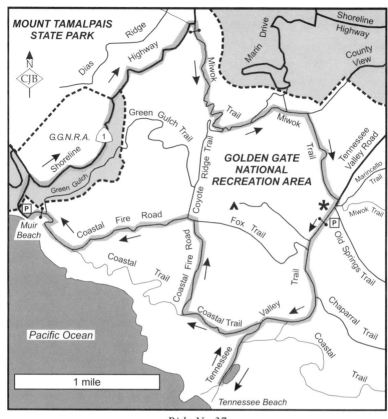

MOUNT TAMALPAIS STATE PARK

Dias

Ridge

Highway

Green Gulch Trail

G.G.N.R.A. 1

Shoreline

Green Gulch

P

Muir Beach

Coastal Fire Road

Coastal Trail

Coastal Fire Road

Pacific Ocean

Coastal Trail

Tennessee

Tennessee Beach

N CJB

Miwok Trail

Marin Drive

Shoreline Highway

County View

Miwok Trail

GOLDEN GATE NATIONAL RECREATION AREA

Tennessee Valley Road

Marincello Trail

Coyote Ridge Trail

Fox Trail

*

P

Old Springs Trail

Miwok Trail

Valley Trail

Chaparral Trail

Coastal Trail

1 mile

Ride No.37

Miwok Trail with Angel Island in the background

38 Mill Valley
Mt. Tamalpais — East Peak Loop

Difficulty Rating: *Moderate*	**Total Distance:** *12 miles*
Skill Level: *Somewhat technical*	**Off-Road Distance:** *12 miles*
Elevation Gain: *1,500 feet*	**Riding Time:** *2-3 hours*

About the Ride

The boom in the mountain biking had its birth in the hills around Mt. Tamalpais in Marin County. The all-terrain bike was first developed here by hiking and bicycling enthusiasts who saw the need for a rugged and durable bike and who had the vision of what it would lead to. While accessible on foot, the many trails around Mt. Tamalpais became wildly popular with the advent of the mountain bike.

This ride consists of a loop around Mt. Tamalpais East Peak, the highest point in the park, rising to an elevation of 2,570 feet. It follows some of the most popular trails in the park, used by hikers and equestrians alike, as well as cyclists. Use caution, avoid excessive speeds and be courteous to others along the trail. The route begins at Mountain Home Inn on Panoramic Highway, near the town of Mill Valley. On weekends the parking lot fills early, so it may be necessary to park along the road nearby and to ride to the start point.

The route initially follows Gravity Car Grade, a generally flat fire road leading to the main loop. Hoo-Koo-E-Koo Road winds along the ridge to connect with Indian Road and then Eldridge Grade for the main climb in the ride. Indian Road and Eldridge Grade are both somewhat steep and a bit bumpy, but a slow and steady pace will get you to the top. You can expect views to Lake Lagunitas and Bon Tempe Lake along the top part of Eldridge Grade. At the top of the mountain is a parking area with restrooms and views of the surrounding landscapes. From there, the route descends along Old Railroad Grade and passes by West Point Inn, a popular gathering place for cyclists, hikers and equestrians. The return to the staring point is again along Old Railroad Grade and finally along Gravity Car Grade.

The trails are generally wide and smooth. Indian Grade and Eldridge Grade are steep and bumpy. Bicycle speed limits are 15 miles per hour and are strictly enforced.

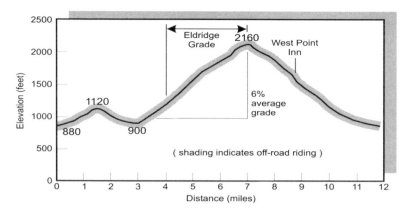

Starting Point

Start the ride at the main parking lot on Panoramic Highway at Mountain Home Inn. To get there, take Highway 101 to southern Marin County and get off at the exit for Highway 1 and Stinson Beach. Follow Highway 1 (Shoreline Highway) for about 3 miles and turn right onto Panoramic Highway. The parking lot and Mountain Home Inn are 2-3 miles up the road.

Mile Markers

0.0 Proceed from the parking area and cross the road onto the paved road. Bear RIGHT to get on a dirt road leading into the Mt. Tamalpais Watershed area and continue past the gate.

1.0 Bear LEFT at the trail split onto Old Railroad Grade and then continue STRAIGHT at the trail intersection on the right side shortly after that.

1.4 Turn RIGHT onto Hoo-Koo-E-Koo Road.

3.4 Turn LEFT onto Blithedale Ridge Road and then LEFT again onto Indian Road.

4.1 Turn LEFT onto Eldridge Grade and prepare for a steep and bumpy climb.

6.7 The trail end at the paved road. The top of the mountain is in the parking area to the left. To continue along the route, turn RIGHT on the paved road and look for the trailhead on the far side of the road a short distance ahead. Proceed along this trail, Old Railroad Grade.

8.7 Historic West Point Inn on the left side. Snacks and beverages are available here. Continue past the inn along Old Railroad Grade.

9.5 Intersection with Hogback Road on the right side.

10.3 Intersection with Hoo-Koo-E-Koo Road on the left side.

10.7 Continue STRAIGHT at the trail intersection on the left side and proceed toward Mountain Home Inn.

11.8 End of the ride at the parking area.

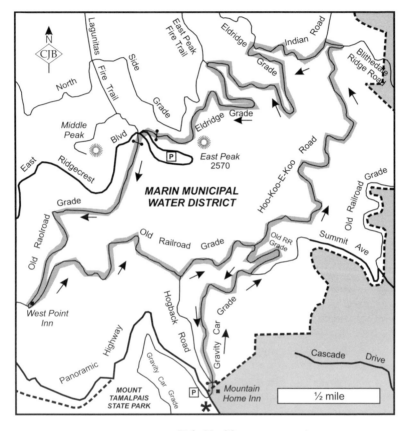

Ride No.38

39 Ross
Mt. Tamalpais Watershed — Lakes Loop

Difficulty Rating: *Moderate*	**Total Distance:** *11 miles*
Skill Level: *Somewhat technical*	**Off-Road Distance:** *9 miles*
Elevation Gain: *1,100 feet*	**Riding Time:** *2 hours*

About the Ride

Water for residents and businesses in Marin County comes from the reservoirs in *Mt. Tamalpais Watershed*, located just to the north of majestic Mt. Tamalpais. Administered by the *Marin Municipal Water District* (MMWD), the lakes are ringed by a network of trails and fire roads leading through the surrounding woodlands and across the rolling hills.

This ride leads past several of the lakes in the watershed. Staring at Greene Park near the town of Ross, the route leads first along a fire road up to Phoenix Lake and then up Shaver Grade to the major trail intersection called Four Corners. Shaver Grade continues climbing after Four Corners, leading to its end point at Sky Oaks Road. A brief stretch on the road leads to the trailhead for Bullfrog Road, which will take you to Bon Tempe Lake and then on to pristine Lake Lagunitas. After circling Lake Lagunitas along its wooded shoreline, the route follows more fire roads for the return to Phoenix Lake and then Greene Park.

The trails are all wide, not very steep and generally smooth. They are not always well-marked and sometimes not even named, so it is important to follow the route directions closely.

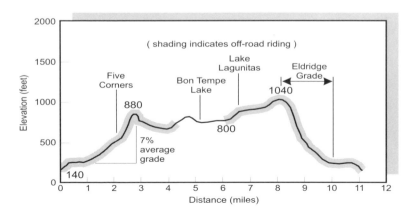

Starting Point

Start the ride in *Natalie Coffin Greene Park* in Ross. To get there, take Highway 101 to Marin County and get off at the exit for Sir Francis Drake Boulevard. Follow Sir Francis Drake Boulevard west for about 3 miles and look for Lagunitas Road on the left side. Turn left onto Lagunitas Road and follow it to its end where Greene Park is located.

Mile Markers

0.0   Proceed WEST out of the parking lot along the paved road.

0.3   Continue STRAIGHT around the right side of Phoenix Lake.

1.0   At Phoenix Junction, bear RIGHT onto Shaver Grade.

2.1   At Five Corners turn LEFT sharply to continue uphill on Shaver Grade.

2.7   At the end of the fire road, turn RIGHT onto the paved road.

3.0   Just before the Sky Oaks Ranger Station on the right side, turn LEFT onto the fire road and bear LEFT at the trail split almost immediately.

3.9   Continue past the gate onto the gravel road.

4.0   Parking area on the right side with trail to Bon Tempe Lake.

4.5   Turn RIGHT onto the paved road.

5.2   Bon Tempe Lake on the right side.

5.7   At the "T" intersection, turn RIGHT toward Lake Lagunitas.

5.9   At the parking lot and picnic area, continue on the trailhead located on the right side of the parking area. This is Rock Springs – Lagunitas Road

6.3   Lake Lagunitas is on the left side.

6.4   Bear LEFT to continue around the lake. Rock Springs – Lagunitas Road branches off to the right.

7.3   Cross a bridge and turn RIGHT at the "T" intersection onto unmarked fire road.

8.0   Turn LEFT onto Eldridge Grade and begin descent.

8.8   Continue STRAIGHT at the trail intersection on the right side.

9.3   Turn RIGHT at unmarked trail junction to continue descent along Eldridge Grade.

10.1   Back at Phoenix Junction, turn RIGHT onto Shaver Grade, heading toward Phoenix Lake.

10.4   Phoenix Lake on the right side.

11.1   End of the ride at the parking area.

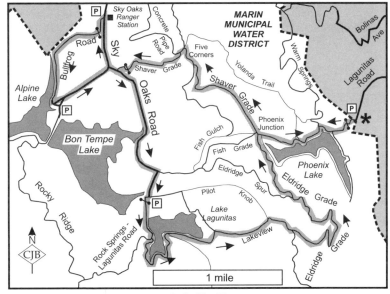

Ride No.39

40 Muir Beach
Mt. Tamalpais and Muir Woods

Difficulty Rating: *Moderate*   **Total Distance:** *9 miles*
Skill Level: *Somewhat technical* **Off-Road Distance:** *5 miles*
Elevation Gain: *1,300 feet*   **Riding Time:** *2 hours*

About the Ride

Just north of San Francisco stands one of the impressive groves of ancient redwoods in the Bay Area. *Muir Woods National Monument* has long beckoned visitors with its giant trees and secluded trails. The density of the forest in Muir Woods contrasts sharply with nearby *Mt. Tamalpais State Park*, characterized by grassy slopes and rugged peaks. Whereas Mt. Tam has numerous trails open to mountain bikes, Muir Woods does not, with the exception of Deer Park Fire Road on its periphery.

This ride consists of a loop through *Mt. Tamalpais State Park* and along Deer Park Fire Road. The route begins at sea level at Muir Beach and initially leads up along Muir Woods Road for about 2 miles toward Muir Woods. Turning off the pavement onto Deer Park Fire Road, you will continue to climb until you reach the high point at "Cardiac Hill". The descent back to Highway 1 is along Coastal Trail with dramatic views of the ocean. A short downhill stretch of about 1½ miles along Highway 1 will bring you back to Muir Beach.

Deer Park Fire Road generally follows parallel to Dipsea Trail and the trails cross each other several times. Dipsea Trail is a trail popular with runners and hikers. While Deer Park Fire Road is wide and smooth, Coastal Trail is quite bumpy and steep. The final downhill section along Highway 1 can be busy with car traffic, so careful riding is important.

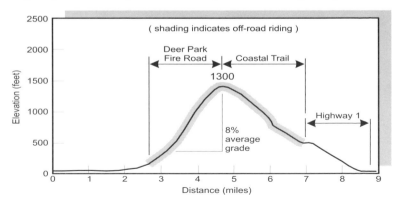

Starting Point

Start the ride at Muir Beach, just off Highway 1. To get there, take Highway 1 north from San Francisco or south from northern Marin County. Look for the Pelican Inn at the intersection with Muir Woods Road. Muir Beach is just down the road and has parking and restrooms.

Mile Markers

- 0.0 Proceed out of the Muir Beach parking area toward Highway 1.
- 0.3 Turn LEFT onto Highway 1 (Shoreline Highway).
- 0.5 Bear RIGHT to get on Muir Woods Road.
- 2.4 Turn LEFT onto Deer Park Fire Road — trail marker at the gate indicates Old Mine Trail.
- 4.5 Ben Johnson Trail intersection on the right side.
- 4.9 Turn LEFT onto Coastal Trail.
- 7.0 Continue STRAIGHT past the gate — Heather Cutoff is to the left.
- 7.3 At the end of the trail, turn LEFT onto Highway 1.
- 7.7 Muir Beach overlook on the right side.
- 8.7 Continue STRAIGHT at the intersection with Muir Woods Road on the left to stay on Highway 1.
- 9.0 Turn RIGHT at the Pelican Inn onto Pacific Way towards Muir Beach.
- 9.3 End of the ride at Muir Beach parking area.

View from the top of "Cardiac Hill"

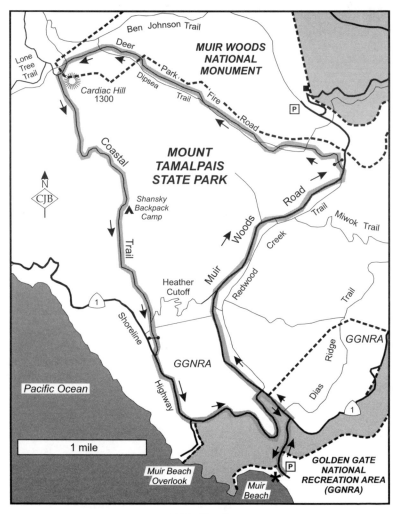

Ride No.40

41 San Rafael

China Camp State Park

Difficulty Rating: *Moderate*	**Total Distance:** *9 miles*
Skill Level: *Somewhat technical*	**Off-Road Distance:** *9 miles*
Elevation Gain: *700 feet*	**Riding Time:** *2 hours*

About the Ride

In the late 1800's, Chinese immigrants living in San Francisco suffered many indignations caused by the prejudice that was prevalent there at that time. Many of them relocated across the bay to Marin and settled in an area along the shoreline that was convenient for their shrimp-harvesting trade. Today that area is known as *China Camp State Park* and is a popular destination for overnight campers and mountain bike enthusiasts. While most state parks in California permit mountain biking only along fire roads, China Camp is a notable exception. All the single-track trails in the park are legal for bikes and this is a major factor in the park's popularity for cyclists.

The route of this ride initially leads up a steep incline along Bay View Trail to get to the higher ridges in the park. Once the main climb is out of the way, the route leads along shady single-track on a slightly uphill grade and then begins the long downhill. The gentle grades ensure that the downhill lasts a long time. First continuing along Bay View Trail and then following along Oak Ridge Trail, this part of the ride offers views in both directions. The end of Oak Ridge Trail is at the far end of the park and leads to Shoreline Trail for the relatively flat return.

While the main climb in the beginning is not terribly high, it is steep. Once up the hill, however, the ride becomes a very enjoyable cruise along narrow and bumpy single-track.

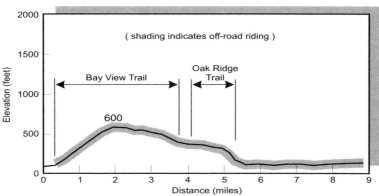

Starting Point

Begin the ride at the main parking area in *China Camp State Park*. To get there, take Highway 101 to San Rafael in Marin County and get off at the exit for North San Pedro Road. Head east on North San Pedro Road, following the signs for China Camp. Go into the park at the first entrance and go to the end of the paved road where there is a large parking area.

Mile Markers

0.0   From the main parking area, proceed back down the paved road toward the main entrance of the park where you came in.

0.2   Turn LEFT into the day-use parking area and continue STRAIGHT through on the Bay View Trail.

0.4   Continue STRAIGHT at the trail intersections on both sides.

0.7   Trail intersection on the right side with a view point straight ahead. Bear LEFT to stay on Bay View Trail

0.8   Bear RIGHT to continue along Bay View Trail toward Back Ranch Trail.

1.7   Veer LEFT and cross a bridge — Echo Trail is to the right.

2.3   Cross under power lines and turn LEFT onto Back Ranch Fire Trail. Then bear RIGHT to resume Bay View Trail.

3.7   Turn LEFT onto Miwok Fire Trail.

4.0   Bear LEFT to stay on Miwok Fire Trail and then make an immediate RIGHT to get on Oak Ridge Trail.

4.3   Continue STRAIGHT across McNears Fire Trail to stay on Oak Ridge Trail.

4.6   Continue STRAIGHT across McNears Fire Trail again to stay on Oak Ridge Trail. To the right is a good view point at the top of a small hill.

5.2   Turn LEFT onto Peacock Gap Trail, which runs parallel to a paved road.

5.4   Continue STRAIGHT on Shoreline Trail as Peacock Trail branches to the right. Cross bridge.

7.0   Cross another bridge.

7.2   Continue STRAIGHT across Miwok Fire Trail to stay on Shoreline Trail.

7.6   Continue through the parking lot for Miwok Meadows day-use area and continue on Shoreline Trail. Cross bridge

8.1   Bear LEFT to stay on Shoreline Trail — Bullet Hill Trail is to the right.

8.4   Bear LEFT to stay on Shoreline Trail — North San Pedro Road is to the right.

8.6 Bear LEFT and then RIGHT to head toward the main parking area visible straight ahead.

8.7 Continue through the campground and then turn RIGHT to cross a bridge back to the main parking area.

8.9 End of the ride at the parking area.

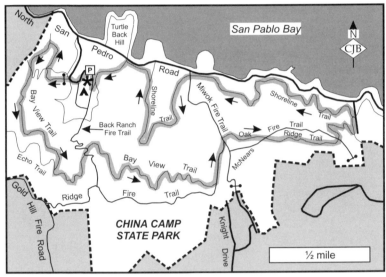

Ride No.41

View from Oak Ridge Trail

42 Olema
Bolinas Ridge and Point Reyes

Difficulty Rating: *Difficult*	**Total Distance:** *27 miles*
Skill Level: *Very technical*	**Off-Road Distance:** *16 miles*
Elevation Gain: *2,300 feet*	**Riding Time:** *3-4 hours*

About the Ride

Running parallel to Highway 1 in a north-south direction, the Bolinas Ridge Trail follows along the top of the inland mountain range stretching from Bolinas north to Olema, near Point Reyes. Expansive views of Bolinas Lagoon in the south and Tomales Bay in the north make this trail one of the more beautiful ones to ride on in the North Bay area. Just to the west of Bolinas Ridge Trail and across Highway 1 lies *Point Reyes National Seashore*. While Point Reyes has only a small number of trails on which bikes are permitted, there is one trail, Olema Valley Trail, running parallel to Highway 1, which can be conveniently tied in to the Bolinas Ridge Trail to make a challenging and interesting loop.

The route starts in Olema near the turn-off for the Point Reyes visitor center and park headquarters. After heading south on Highway 1 for about 4 miles, you will then turn into the Five Brooks parking area and get on Olema Valley Trail. Leading through the inland forests and some open meadows on some very challenging single-track, the trail returns to Highway 1 just north of Bolinas. You will then follow Highway 1 south to Fairfax-Bolinas Road for the climb to reach the trailhead for Bolinas Ridge Trail. After some ups and downs, Bolinas Ridge Trail follows a steady descent through pastures and woods until it ends at Sir Francis Drake Boulevard for the easy return to Olema.

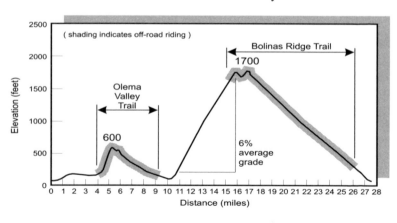

Starting Point

Start the ride in Olema at the intersection of Highway 1 and Sir Francis Drake Boulevard. To get there, take Highway 101 north from San Francisco and get off at the exit for Sir Francis Drake Boulevard. Follow Sir Francis Drake Boulevard west all the way to its end at Highway 1 in Olema.

Mile Markers

0.0 Proceed SOUTH along Highway 1 away from Olema.

3.6 Turn RIGHT into Five Brooks staging area and continue to the parking area at the end of the road.

3.9 Proceed toward Five Brooks Trail and turn LEFT onto a small unmarked trail just out of the parking area. This will take you to Olema Valley Trail.

4.0 Bear LEFT at the trail split.

5.3 Bolema Trail intersection on the right side.

6.6 Bear RIGHT to stay on Olema Valley Trail.

8.9 Texeira Trail intersection on the right side.

9.4 Turn RIGHT onto Highway 1 at the end of Olema Valley Trail.

10.6 Turn LEFT onto Fairfax-Bolinas Road and begin climbing.

15.1 Turn LEFT onto Bolinas Ridge Trail at the top of the hill.

16.9 High point of the ride at 1,700 feet.

19.8 Randall Trail intersection on the left side.

20.9 Shafter Trail intersection on the right side.

24.7 Bear LEFT at the intersection with Jewell Trail on the right side to stay on Bolinas Ridge Trail.

26.1 Continue past the gate and turn LEFT onto Sir Francis Drake Boulevard.

27.3 End of the ride back in Olema.

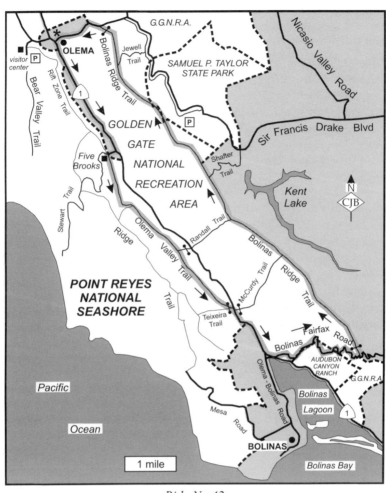

Ride No.42

43 Olema

Point Reyes National Seashore Bike & Hike

Difficulty Rating: *Easy*	**Total Bike Distance:** *6 miles*
Skill Level: *Non technical*	**Total Hike Distance:** *3 miles*
Bike Elevation Gain: *500 feet*	**Riding Time:** *1 hours*
Hike Elevation Gain: *200 feet*	**Hiking Time:** *1-2 hours*

About the Ride

Point Reyes National Seashore has only a few trails legal for bikes to use. The vast majority of the park is dedicated to hikers and equestrians. This ride presents a great opportunity to combine an easy bike ride with a hike. The reward is to get access to some spots in the park that are very difficult to get to otherwise.

The route for the bike ride is quite simple, leading directly away from the visitor center in Olema along Bear Valley Trail. The trail is a wide fire road and is shady and usually quite smooth. Although there is a small hill to get over, the grade is gentle and can be handled by just about anyone.

At the end of Bear Valley Trail, a rack is provided for storing and locking bikes. Be sure to bring along a lock if you plan to do the hike. Sturdy hiking shoes will be necessary as well, as the trails can be difficult to hike in biking shoes. To get the full Point Reyes experience, bring along a picnic and a blanket as there a numerous places to stop along the shoreline. There are several trail options. The two that are suggested are an easy out-and-back to the shoreline and a more difficult loop which goes to some more isolated places.

Starting Point

Start the ride at the *Point Reyes National Seashore* park headquarters and visitor center in Olema. To get there, take Highway 101 north from San Francisco and get off at the exit for Sir Francis Drake Boulevard. Follow Sir Francis Drake Boulevard west all the way to its end at Highway 1 in Olema. Turn right onto Highway 1 and then left onto Bear Valley Road. Follow the signs for the visitor center. Be sure to check out the visitor center, which has interesting information about Point Reyes.

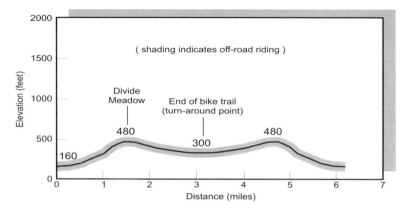

Mile Markers

0.0   Proceed past the visitor center along the road. Continue past the gate along Bear Valley Trail.

0.2   Sky Trail intersection on the right side.

0.8   Meadow Trail intersection on the right side.

1.5   Divide Meadow — highest point in the ride — Old Pine Trail intersection on the right side.

3.2   End of the bicycle trail. Lock your bike to the bike rack and do the hike from here. Return back to the visitor center the way you came.

6.4   End of the ride back at the visitor center.

Easy Hike

Out-and-back along Bear Valley Trail to Arch Rock — about 1.8 miles round-trip.

Longer Hike

Follow Baldy Trail, Sky Trail, Coast Trail and Glen Trail — about 5.6 miles total.

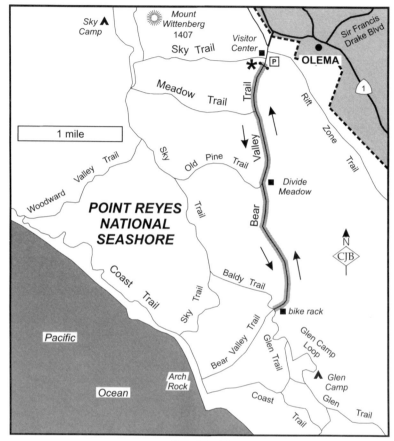

Ride No.43

44 Lagunitas
Samuel P. Taylor State Park
and Bolinas Ridge Loop

Difficulty Rating: *Moderate*	**Total Distance:** *14 miles*
Skill Level: *Somewhat technical*	**Off-Road Distance:** *12 miles*
Elevation Gain: *1,200 feet*	**Riding Time:** *3 hours*

About the Ride

The redwood groves along the tranquil Papermill Creek in *Samuel P. Taylor State Park* and the grassy slopes of Bolinas Ridge high above make the terrain of this ride a study in contrasts. The route begins just inside the park entrance on Sir Francis Drake Boulevard, just west of the township of Lagunitas. It initially follows an access road through the park and continues along a paved bike path along the creek. The peace and quiet and the beauty of the majestic redwood forest provide a calm backdrop for this gentle warm-up.

The bike path ends at Sir Francis Drake Boulevard and the warm-up is over as the route leads uphill on the road to the trailhead for the Bolinas Ridge Trail. A wide fire road, Bolinas Ridge Trail has views of Point Reyes to the west as it climbs steadily along a grade that is not very steep. The route comes down off the ridge along Shafter Bridge Fire Road, a very steep downhill that will require hard braking most of the way down. You get back to the park entrance first along Sir Francis Drake Boulevard and then along a gravel bike path.

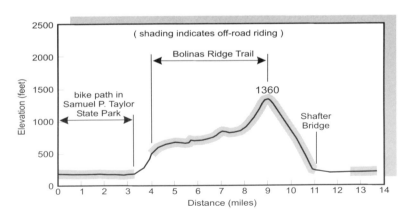

Starting Point

Begin the ride at *Samuel P. Taylor State Park.* To get there, take Highway 101 to southern Marin County and get off at Sir Francis Drake Boulevard. Follow Sir Francis Drake Boulevard about 16 miles west to the park. Begin the ride inside the park near the park entrance.

Mile Markers

0.0 Proceed into the park along the road leading from the park entrance.

0.1 Cross over a bridge and then turn RIGHT onto the main access road leading through the park.

1.2 Continue past the gate onto the bike path.

3.4 Just before the road under-crossing, turn LEFT on a gravel path and then turn LEFT onto Sir Francis Drake Boulevard.

4.1 At the top of the hill, turn LEFT and go past the gate to get on Bolinas Ridge Trail.

5.2 Livestock gate.

5.5 Bear RIGHT to stay on Bolinas Ridge Trail at the intersection with Jewell Trail on the left side.

9.3 Turn LEFT onto unmarked Shafter Fire Road and begin a steep descent.

10.7 At the bottom, turn LEFT onto a gravel trail.

11.2 At the end of the trail, turn LEFT onto Sir Francis Drake Boulevard.

12.5 Cross over bridge on the main road and then look for the bike path on the right side. Turn RIGHT and then LEFT to get on the bike path.

13.3 Back on the paved road in the park, turn RIGHT and cross bridge toward the park entrance.

13.4 End of the ride at the park entrance.

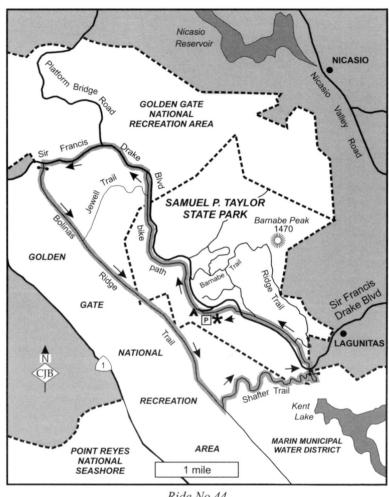

Ride No.44

45   Santa Rosa
Annadel State Park

Difficulty Rating: *Moderate*	**Total Distance:** *14 miles*
Skill Level: *Somewhat technical*	**Off-Road Distance:** *14 miles*
Elevation Gain: *1,300 feet*	**Riding Time:** *2-3 hours*

About the Ride

About 60 miles north of San Francisco and just outside of Santa Rosa lies one of the most popular mountain bike destinations in the North Bay. *Annadel State Park*, encompassing some 5,000 acres of redwoods, oaks, manzanita and scrub brush, has terrain and scenery to both inspire and to challenge. While the elevations don't match those of the higher coastal mountains and the trails aren't particularly steep, the numerous rocky sections make the going quite rough in many places. Tricky climbs and bone-jarring descents offer the main challenges in Annadel. The rewards are the diverse scenery and the stunning views.

This ride offers a fairly complete tour of the park and includes loops around both Lake Ilsanjo and Ledson Marsh. The route leads from the main parking area uphill along smooth and shady W.P. Richardson Trail. A short stretch on single-track along Louis Trail is followed by a bumpy section on North Burma Trail and a smooth cruise through a pleasant meadow along Live Oak Trail. After looping around tranquil Lake Ilsanjo, the route leads to the main climb, first on bumpy Marsh Trail and then along Ridge Trail.

The route around Ledson Marsh is flat and smooth. The best time to view the wildlife in the marsh is in the spring after the winter rains. The marsh dries up in the summer but is always a peaceful place to visit. The return follows once again along Marsh Trail and then the fun begins on the hairy descent along rugged South Burma Trail. The final section of the ride again follows along W.P. Richardson Trail.

Starting Point

To get to *Annadel State Park*, take Highway 101 to Santa Rosa and get off at the exit for Highway 12. Follow Highway 12 east as it leads through Santa Rosa. After about 4 miles, turn right onto Mission Boulevard and then left onto Montgomery Drive. Follow Montgomery Drive for another 1½ miles to Channel Drive. Park in the parking area at the end of Channel Drive.

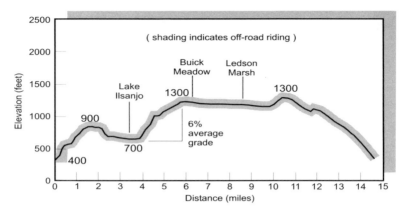

Mile Markers

0.0 Proceed into the park along Warren P. Richardson Trail.

1.5 Turn RIGHT onto Louis Trail.

1.9 Turn RIGHT onto North Burma Trail.

2.3 Turn LEFT onto Live Oak Trail.

2.6 Continue STRAIGHT onto Rough Go Trail. There are six trail merging at this point, so be sure to take the one straight ahead.

3.3 Bear LEFT to stay on Rough Go Trail and continue across the dam toward Lake Ilsanjo.

3.5 Turn RIGHT onto Canyon Trail.

4.1 Turn LEFT onto Marsh Trail and begin climbing.

6.1 Bear RIGHT to stay on Marsh Trail at Buick Meadow.

6.4 Turn RIGHT onto Ridge Trail.

7.8 Turn LEFT onto Marsh Trail.

8.1 Continue STRAIGHT at the intersection with Pig Flat Trail on the right side and wind around the marsh.

9.1 Bear LEFT to stay on Marsh Trail at the intersection with Two Quarry Trail on the right side.

9.5 Ridge Trail intersection on the left side.

9.8 Turn RIGHT onto South Burma Trail.

12.2 Turn RIGHT onto Warren P. Richardson Trail.

12.4 Bear RIGHT to stay on Warren P. Richardson Trail.

13.6 Two Quarry Trail intersection on the right side.

14.4 End of the ride at the parking area.

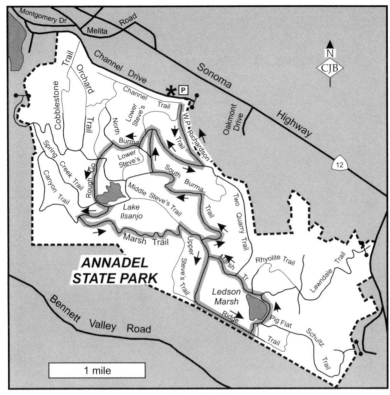

Ride No.45

Lake Ilsanjo in Annadel State Park

APPENDIX

RIDES BY RATINGS

Ride No.	Ride Name	Miles	Elevation	Page No.
EASY RIDES with Non-Technical Skills				
6.	Forest of Nisene Marks State Park — Five Finger Falls Bike & Hike	8	500	27
9.	Henry Cowell Redwoods State Park	6	700	37
10.	Big Basin — Berry Creek Falls Bike & Hike	12	400	40
20.	Old Haul Road	16	800	73
28.	Coyote Hills Regional Park	15	100	98
29.	Morgan Territory Regional Preserve	7	600	101
35.	Angel Island State Park	11	700	121
43.	Point Reyes National Seashore Bike & Hike	6	500	145
EASY RIDES with Somewhat Technical skills				
14.	Arastradero Preserve	5	600	55
MODERATE RIDES with Non-Technical Skills				
7.	Forest of Nisene Marks — Sand Point Overlook	18	1400	32
11.	Big Basin Redwoods State Park	16	1500	44
MODERATE RIDES with Somewhat Technical Skills				
2.	St. Joseph's Hill Open Space Preserve	6	700	14
13.	Wilder Ranch, UCSC, and Pogoip Preserve	16	1600	51
16.	Fremont Older Open Space Preserve	6	1300	61
17.	Butano State Park	12	2000	64
21.	Russian Ridge Open Space Preserve	11	1300	76
22.	Skyline Ridge Open Space Preserve	7	1200	79
23.	Saratoga Gap and Long Ridge Preserves	10	900	82
26.	Redwood Regional Park	10	1200	92
32.	Tilden Park and Wildcat Canyon Regional Parks	17	1700	110
38.	Mt. Tamalpais — East Peak Loop	12	1500	130
39.	Mt. Tamalpais Watershed — Lakes Loop	11	1100	133
40.	Mt. Tamalpais and Muir Woods	9	1300	136
41.	China Camp State Park	9	700	139
44.	Samuel P. Taylor State Park and Bolinas Ridge Loop	14	1200	148
45.	Annadel State Park	14	1300	151

Ride No.	Ride Name	Miles	Elevation	Page No.
DIFFICULT RIDES with Somewhat Technical Skills				
1.	Grant Ranch County Park	16	1900	11
3.	Sierra Azul Open Space Preserve	16	3000	17
5.	Henry Coe State Park — Wilson Ranch Loop	17	2000	23
15.	Monte Bello Open Space Preserve	17	2500	58
24.	Alpine Road and Windy Hill	18	2200	85
25.	Anthony Chabot Regional Park	20	2200	89
27.	Pleasanton Ridge Regional Park	9	1600	95
30.	Sunol-Ohlone Regional Wilderness	10	2000	104
31.	Briones Regional Park	10	1700	107
33.	Mt. Diablo — Wall Point Road	9	1800	114
36.	Marin Headlands	24	2800	124
37.	Tennessee Valley and Muir Beach	11	1700	127
DIFFICULT RIDES with Very Technical Skills				
4.	Henry Coe State Park — Middle Ridge Loop	10	2100	20
8.	Soquel Demonstration Forest	13	1900	34
12.	Wilder Ranch State Park	13	1600	48
18.	El Corte de Madera Open Space Preserve	10	2200	67
19.	Purisima Creek Redwoods	9	1600	70
34.	Mt. Diablo — Mitchell Canyon	9	1900	117
42.	Bolinas Ridge and Point Reyes	27	2300	142

Spring flowers at Wilder Ranch State Park

BICYCLING TIPS

Familiarize yourself with these simple tips to become a better and safer cyclist.

General Rules and Tips for Off-Road Riding

1. Know the rules for the area in which you are riding. Always stay on trails intended for bikes. Leave the area just as you found it.
2. Yield to equestrians. Horses may spook when a bicycle appears suddenly. When approaching from behind, talk loudly so the horse can hear you coming. Most horses are familiar with human voices, but not with bicycles.
3. Slow down when you approach hikers. It is important to share the trails harmoniously. A simple bell mounted on the handlebar is a nice way to signal your approach.
4. Always be courteous. Nothing is worse for the sport than hostility between trail users.
5. Look ahead to anticipate encounters. Approach blind curves slowly.
6. Avoid contact with plant life along the trails. Poison oak is very common in northern California and can be a very unpleasant experience.
7. Mountain bike tires can be deflated a small amount to provide for better traction in loose conditions.
8. Whenever you dismount, be sure to get out of the way and to not impede others.
9. When riding in a group, it is both safe and polite to regroup frequently. Avoid getting spread out over long distances.

Mountain Biking Techniques

1. A properly adjusted saddle height will ensure your comfort and will help to avoid knee injuries. The correct height will result in a slight bend in the knee when the leg is in its fully extended position on the lower of the two pedals.
2. Be familiar with gear shifting so you can anticipate the hills and shift before you need to. It can be difficult to shift when there is a lot of pressure on the pedals and the chain can come off in these conditions. Always continue to pedal while shifting.

3. If you are using clipless pedals or toe clips, try pulling up on the pedals as well as pushing down. This uses different muscles and can give you better efficiency.

4. When descending along steep trails, stop and lower your saddle before you begin the descent. This lowers your center of gravity and makes it easier to dismount or to put a foot down, thus making it considerably safer. More skilled riders will be able to stretch out from the handlebars so that their back ends are beyond the back of the saddle and even almost touching the top of the rear wheels.

5. Use your front brake more than your rear one on steep descents. There is much more weight on your front wheel going downhill and braking too much on the rear brakes can cause skidding and loss of control.

6. Don't focus on a particular rock or hazard ahead of you, since that will tend to make you ride directly toward it. It is better to focus on the path you want to take around the hazard.

7. Avoid the temptation to stand on steep climbs. This reduces the weight on the rear wheel and usually causes it to lose traction. Better to stay down and gut it out.

8. When descending on a bumpy and hazardous trail, be confident that the bike will roll over obstacles. Look ahead on the trail to pick the track you want to follow and allow the bike to roll there. Try to avoid braking hard as the bike hits an obstacle. It is better to roll over it and to brake when you are in an area with good traction.

9. When descending along a bumpy trail, get out of the saddle and ride with both pedal arms parallel to the ground. Hold the saddle firmly between your thighs and use that to control the sideways movement of the bike.

10. Riding in sand or loose dirt is especially difficult. If you can shift your weight from the front wheel to the back, this will allow the bike to float over the sand a bit and give you more control.

Equipment

1. Always wear a helmet.

2. Wear goggles or some other form of eyewear to protect your eyes from the harmful effects of the sun and from dirt and debris that may be present.

3. Carry maps at all times, unless you are very familiar with the area.

4. Be sure to take along adequate water and stay hydrated, especially on hot days. Hydration systems offer large water capacity and keep the water readily available while riding.

5. Verify the operation of your bike *before* you begin the ride.

6. Always carry at least a spare tube, patch kit, tire pump and tire irons. Allen wrenches and a chain tool can also save the day in emergencies.

7. Be prepared to fix your own problems. Don't count on someone coming along to help.

8. Wear goggles or some other form of eyewear to protect your eyes from the harmful effects of the sun and from dirt and debris that may be present.

ABOUT THE AUTHOR

Born in New Jersey, Conrad Boisvert has been a resident of northern California since 1972. With a long career as a microelectronics engineer, he has been a recreational cyclist for many years. Not only has he toured the many roads and trails in and around the Bay Area, but he has also cycled throughout the continental United States and in Hawaii, Alaska, Canada, Mexico, Costa Rica, New Zealand, Bali, Ireland, France, Italy, and Austria. He is the author of three other bicycle guide books and currently resides in Aptos and in the Sierras.

THE BAY AREA BIKE TRAILS SERIES

The Bay Area Bike Trails Series offers over 185 self-guided road and mountain bicycle tours. Each ride contains clear, detailed maps, easily followed directions with mile markers, elevation profiles of the terrain, beautiful photographs, historical background and points of interest.

Bay Area Mountain Bike Trails, 2nd Edition by Conrad J. Boisvert, 2004. $18.95. The Bay Area offers some of the most exciting and scenic off-road trails and a wealth of hidden trails, all within easy access of major cities. From Santa Rosa south to Gilroy, you can ride along the spectacular ridges of Mt. Tamalpais, view the Golden Gate Bridge from the Marin Headlands, or challenge yourself on the hills of Mt. Diablo.

East Bay Bike Trails by Conrad J. Boisvert, 1992 (latest revision 2002). $15.95. Somewhat sheltered from coastal fog and ocean winds, the East Bay extends from the Carquinez Strait south to Fremont. Interesting bike routes take you through heavily wooded hills above Oakland and Berkeley, orchards and farms around Brentwood, eerie windmills in Livermore, the wetlands around Newark, and dramatic Mt. Diablo in Danville.

Marin County Bike Trails by Phyllis L. Neumann, 1989 (latest revision 2001). $15.95. Just across the Golden Gate Bridge, Marin County combines exquisite natural beauty with sophisticated elegance to give you spectacular views, rugged cliffs, natural beaches, well-developed parks, rural farmlands, tiny hidden towns and Mt. Tamalpais. A specially designed bike route from Petaluma to the Golden Gate Bridge is also included.

San Francisco Peninsula Bike Trails, by Conrad J. Boisvert, 1991 (latest revision 2001). $14.95. Few areas can compare with the spectacular San Francisco Peninsula, which encompasses the wooded foothills around Woodside, dense redwood forests in the Santa Cruz mountains and remote country roads along the rugged Pacific coastline.

Sonoma County Bike Trails, 3rd Edition by Phyllis L. Neumann, 1999 (latest revision 2001). $15.95. Less than an hour's drive north from San Francisco brings you to tranquil country roads, gently rolling farmlands, towering redwoods, lush vineyards, local wineries, the Russian River and the Pacific coastline. A specially designed bike route from Cloverdale to Petaluma is also included.

South Bay Bike Trails, 2nd Edition by Conrad J. Boisvert, 2000. (latest revision 2001) $15.95. Better known for its high-tech image, once you head out into the surrounding countryside, the South Bay is a cyclist's paradise. From San Jose south to Gilroy, picturesque rides take you through ranchlands around Morgan Hill, dense redwood forests in the Santa Cruz mountains, and the coastal wetlands of the Elkhorn Slough. Heading south along the Pacific coast brings you to the famous seaside resorts and beaches of Santa Cruz and Capitola.